I'm So Sorry

ALSO BY JAMES L. DICKERSON

Dixie Chicks

Last Suppers

North to Canada

Dixie's Dirty Secret

Women on Top

That's Alright, Elvis

Goin' Back to Memphis

Country Music's Most Embarrassing Moments

Coming Home

I'm So Sorry

The Stories Behind
101 Very Public Apologies

JAMES L. DICKERSON

LF LEBHAR-FRIEDMAN BOOKS

NEW YORK · CHICAGO · LOS ANGELES · LONDON · PARIS · TOKYO

Lebhar-Friedman Books
425 Park Avenue
New York, NY 10022

Published by Lebhar-Friedman Books
Lebhar-Friedman Books is a company of Lebhar-Friedman, Inc.

Printed in the United States of America

Library of Congress Cataloging-in-Publication Data
Dickerson, James.
I'm so sorry : the stories behind 101 very public apologies / James L. Dickerson.
p. cm.
Includes index.
ISBN: 0-86730-814-1 (alk. paper)
1. Celebrities—United States—Biography—Miscellanea. 2. Apologizing. I. Title.
CT214.D53 2000
920.02—dc21
00-056343

PHOTO CREDITS

Text design by Tina Thompson

Visit our Web site at lfbooks.com

To everyone I have ever offended, overlooked, or slighted

(and you know who you are)

please accept my most heartfelt apologies

(even if I am totally in the right).

Contents

Acknowledgments

I would like to thank the following people for their help with this book: the staff at the Jean and Alexander Heard Library at Vanderbilt University; my editor, Frank Scatoni; my publisher, Geoff Golson; Arlete Santos at Archive Photos; Douglas Holliday; Sue Moskowitz at Lebhar-Friedman; Pam Gaia, for reminding me of the politics of apology; Martha and Jim McKernan, for leaving a light on near the border; the staff at the Public Library of Nashville and Davidson County; Jim Barkley at National Book Network; and family members who endured my frequent Chinese interpretations of the book title. (*Or-huh-ba-chin*—this is the phonetic rendering of the Chinese term—means "I'm so sorry.")

I'm So Sorry

Introduction

Americans have an insatiable appetite for public apologies. Next to having a good cry, nothing rings our bell quite like receiving a heartfelt apology, especially if the person giving it drives a more expensive car than we do or lives in the big house on the hill or dates Claudia Schiffer or, heaven forbid, marries Nicole Kidman or Sharon Stone.

The more powerful the person offering the apology, the sweeter the sound of the mea culpa to the person receiving it. We love to receive apologies from our bosses, our political leaders, our stuffy neighbors, our ministers, rabbis, or priests, our sports and movie heroes, our political and military leaders, and our editors.

Unfortunately, the reverse is seldom the case. We don't like to issue apologies, especially to the poor, the terminally ill, people who work for us, our bosses and spouses, or people of other races or religions. Least of all do we like to apologize to people we have run over in our cars or accidentally set afire or, as a nation, scalded with napalm.

There is a reason for that.

In the beginning, when the Lord created heaven and earth, he set himself up as the Supreme Arbitrator to whom all apologies flowed. The thinking, apparently, was that the system, to be truly effective, required both a Supreme Arbitrator and a network of Lesser Ones—and it was the job of the Supreme Arbitrator to more or less direct traffic among the sinful Lesser Ones by giving second chances to those considered good investments for new and improved behavior in the future.

Without quibbling over *exactly* when the Old and New Testaments established this particular social transaction as dogma, let's just say that it has been accepted policy for at least two thousand years among Jews and Christians: "Ask and ye shall receive."

Just ask for forgiveness, and the Lord will grant it.

Deny forgiveness to those who seek it—and the Lord will take a dim view of your own requests along those lines. No one in their right mind wants the Lord on their case, so it's better in the long run to just say "yes" to all apologies offered. That may or may not have been a factor in Pope John Paul II's unprecedented apology in March 2000 for the sins of the Catholic Church, but the effect was to transfer the responsibility of forgiveness into the hands of those sinned against.

Part of our fascination with contrition can be traced back to America's early dependence on Christian doctrine in establishing a workable framework for governance. With Christianity built on a foundation of divine forgiveness for mortal sins—God forgives those who ask for forgiveness and mortals are instructed to "forgive those who trespass against" them—it was inevitable that government would appropriate building blocks from that same foundation. As a result, saying "I'm sorry" has been an integral ingredient of both public and private life in America for over two hundred years. When government goes astray, its first line of defense has become the mea culpa, which when uttered with furrowed brow and benign countenance is usually viewed as reason enough to "move on to better things." Another part of that fascination with contrition can probably be traced back to the religious diversity that eventually expanded the nation's bulging social fabric. With the introduction of thousands of Jews, Muslims, Buddhists, et cetera, into the nation's melting pot, first- and second-generation Protestant and Catholic Americans found themselves apologizing on a regular basis for trampling on the religious rights of others.

"Oh, I'm sorry—I didn't know" became a part of daily life.

It is probably no accident that early Christians named their writings "apologies." As early printing presses came into vogue, thus allowing people to write in greater quantity and quality, it became necessary to coin a word for those chosen few who devoted their lives to the written apology. They were called apologists.

In their day, apologists were the equivalent of the NBA superstar—everyone looked up to them. Anyone who could spin a good apology, traverse a court of public opinion with it, and then slam-dunk it into an opponent's basket, was almost always the recipient of public adoration. Cardinal John Henry Newman cashed in on the apology craze in the mid-1880s by titling his autobiography *Apologia Pro Vita Sua*.

Jews never apologized for their religion the way Christians did, but they did incorporate the art of the apology as an integral ingredient in their daily lives. By the twentieth century Jewish comedians had made the apology standard fare in their acts.

"Forgive me for asking, but are you a human being?" the vaudeville comic screamed to his flustered sideman on stage. Phrases such as "Forgive me" and "I'm sorry" became indispensable to the working comic. Steve Martin's "Well, excuuuse me!" was dipped from the same well.

As the nation aged, apologies became an increasingly important dimension of public life. During the twentieth century, apologies were made for violations of the civil rights of African Americans, Japanese Americans, Native Americans, and others. For the past twenty-five years, apologies have gone out to homosexuals, women, the handicapped, the vertically challenged . . . well, the list seems endless.

"I'm sorry" seems to have become an indispensable phrase for communication between the sexes. Who among us has ever had a relationship in which the words "I'm sorry" have not been spoken on a regular basis?

"I'm sorry—I didn't think you would mind if I took the baby-sitter out for drinks!"

"I'm sorry—I thought you understood we would have to share a room!"

"I'm sorry—I thought you liked grilled rattlesnake!"

"I'm sorry—she (he) was so cute, I just couldn't control myself!"

"I'm sorry—I thought I told you yesterday I was sorry!"

"I'm sorry—I love you, I'm just not *in* love with you!"

With all the political and social horrors and repression of the 1950s, is it any wonder that one of the biggest hits of the decade was Brenda Lee's "I'm Sorry," which earned the teenage singer a Grammy and record sales of over 14 million? The song was the perfect vehicle to exploit the turmoil of the times.

Political theorist Jean Bethke Elshtain, writing in *The New Republic*, bemoaned the fact that society in the 1990s had become awash in confession: "There is the proverbial low form on daytime talk shows and the slightly higher form in bookstores. Rectitude, it seems, has given way to 'contrition chic.'"

Today, the apology has been elevated to an art form, as "contrition chic" saturates television and radio talk shows, newspaper columns, and even books. Actor Hugh Grant's *Tonight Show* apology for being arrested with a prostitute has been called one of television's greatest moments. That's a little bit scary when you think about it, but it probably says more about us than it does him.

After it was revealed that he had sucked the toes of a prostitute (among other things), political strategist Dick Morris dutifully stood before every television camera he could find to apologize for his actions. He got a book deal out of it and continues to haunt the talk-show circuit, offering apologies to anyone who will listen.

Incredibly, the very system of apologies that has kept civilization chugging along for the past several thousand years, by offering second chances to those who are worthy of continued social acceptance, is at risk of losing its clout. The phrase "Use it or lose it" hardly applies to apologies. The more a person apologizes, the less meaning it has.

The same applies to groups of apologies. The more often we hear politicians or athletes or movie stars say they are sorry for serious misdeeds, the less respect we have for the professions they represent. So many professional football players have been charged with rape, robbery, assault, and even murder that the National Football League has become a stock source of jokes for late-night television hosts such as Jay Leno and David Letterman. Baseball's Daryl Strawberry has received so many second chances for illegal drug use that it has brought the entire league into disrepute.

Today, is there anything more worthless than a public apology?

The only true apologies are those that offer something of value from the person making the apology. One of the most selfless apologies in this book is an unspoken one. A well-known Hollywood actress was nervous about wearing a see-through dress, so her director cleared the set, sending about one hundred men out into the cold.

That actress could have said, "I'm so sorry," to the men, but it would have been a worthless gesture, for it would have given them nothing of herself. Instead, she offered a sincere apology by going outside and throwing open her coat, thus exposing herself to the shocked men standing in the cold. Now, that's a real apology! Apologies that are accompanied with cash or property settlements or resignations from positions of authority should also be considered genuine and worthy of acceptance.

Two of the worst apologies in history belong to former senator Bob Packwood and ex–Olympic hopeful Tonya Harding. Packwood resigned after being charged with numerous counts of sexual harassment. Harding was linked to that bizarre leg-busting attack against Nancy Kerrigan at the 1994 Lillehammer Olympics. The video-tape image of Kerrigan, crumpled in agony after the attack, crying out "Why me? Why me?" will live forever in television coverage of the Olympics. Both Packwood and Harding used the same words everyone else used in their apologies, but each then qualified their apologies with denials cloaked in confusing syntax. Without saying it outright, they seemed to say, "I'm sorry for not being sorry."

The last two sections of the book include variations on the apology. Sometimes called "anti-apologies," they are, in some instances, more important than traditional apologies. Anyone who says publicly, "I did it, but I'm not apologizing," or "I didn't do it, but I apologize anyway," is offering an apology, because, when you get down to it, the best apologies are always those in which individuals take responsibility, either for the misdeed or for the feelings of others thought to be injured by the misdeeds.

Ironically, one of the first things I noticed while scouring the countryside for heartfelt public apologies is that you almost always find them in the vicinity of money. The wealthier a person is, the more likely he is to resort to the use of a public apology.

Am I saying that people who don't have money lead exemplary lives? Of course not. The poorest among us are capable of every foul deed committed by the wealthiest. The difference is this: The poor hardly ever see the need to issue public apologies. In the first place, judges, juries, bill collectors, repo men, et cetera, do not care if they are sorry or not. Second, there's no money in it for them to say they are sorry, the opposite of which is always true for the rich and the famous.

The only exception, perhaps, involves the crime of murder. If a guilty man or woman says they are sorry for decapitating their neighbor, there is a good chance that a judge or jury will spare them from the death penalty, regardless of the size of their bank account—and they'll apologize because . . . well, you know, no one really wants to be strapped in the electric chair or injected with some type of lethal drug.

We've reached a point where apologies have become a form of currency. We trade them for something we want or for something we don't want to lose. President Bill Clinton traded a public apology for an opportunity to keep his job.

Actually, what we are witnessing today is a significant role reversal, engineered by the political spin doctors of the past three decades. When a professional athlete or an elected official or a business executive stands before you to offer an apology, they are not acknowledging a higher power or a system of moral checks and balances so much as they are manipulating your sense of place in the world.

When Bill Clinton asked for our forgiveness, what he did, in essence, was transfer the power of the Supreme One to us, allowing us to feel we had the power of forgiveness over him. We don't, of course. We forgave him because it made us feel good about ourselves.

Of all the concepts spin doctors have conjured up over the years, this idea of role reversal is probably the most devious. The Lesser Ones among us are so starved for a sense of personal worth that we will offer forgiveness to anyone who asks for it because, for the moment, *it makes us feel like we are important.*

One of the things that struck me once I had collected and assembled the apologies in this book was the realization that, with some notable exceptions, the apologetic people mentioned in these pages represent the brightest, most talented, most daring people of the twentieth century. They come from all walks of life—politics, entertainment, business, the media, sports. Many of them are our heroes.

Sadly, these same people are not always the most honorable and admirable among us. How is it that we have allowed them to assume positions of leadership in business, sports, entertainment, and politics? How is it that when they have abused their positions, we have allowed them to continue as if nothing had happened—and all we ask in return is an apology?

If you've ever wondered what our political and business leaders, and our entertainment and sports heroes, do in their spare time to merit the need for many heartfelt apologies, then all you have to do is keep reading.

You are being offered, within these pages, a collection of the wildest, funniest, dumbest, and most insensitive actions (many of which are beyond the law) that humans are capable of inflicting upon one another. At the end of the day, the best the offenders can do, in most cases, is to say they are sorry.

You will love the people in this book.

You will despise the people in this book.

For those mixed emotions, you will have no one to blame but yourself—and for that I can only say, I'm so sorry.

Chapter 1

The Medium
Is the Message

NBC NEWS
DiMAGGIO'S DEATH GREATLY EXAGGERATED

Baseball legend Joe DiMaggio, affectionately known to his fans as the "Yankee Clipper" and "Joltin' Joe," spent a relaxing evening watching a video of his favorite Western, *Gunfight at the OK Corral*, with his friend Morris Engelberg.

When the movie ended, the television reverted to regular programming. As it happened, the dial was set on NBC, where *Dateline NBC* was in progress. As DiMaggio watched, first in amazement—and then in horror—the following message crawled across the bottom of the television screen:

BASEBALL LEGEND JOE DiMAGGIO HAS DIED AT HIS FLORIDA HOME. HE WAS EIGHTY-FOUR YEARS OLD AND HAD . . .

Abruptly, the message disappeared from the screen.

When he saw the message, DiMaggio was "livid," according to his friend. "Then I made him laugh," Engelberg reported. "I said, 'Joe, we must be in heaven together.'"

NBC blamed the embarrassing mistake on a technician, who pushed the wrong button and inadvertently sent the message out to all the network's East Coast affiliates.

THE APOLOGY

Twenty minutes after the Yankee Clipper's death report appeared, NBC displayed yet another message that corrected the previous message, which it said had been sent in error. NBC executives attempted to telephone DiMaggio to apologize in person, but he would not accept their calls. Instead, they left messages expressing their regret. Less than two months later, the Yankee legend died for real.

CINCINNATI ENQUIRER
FRUIT COMPANY GIVES NEWSPAPER THE SLIP

When the story about Chiquita Brands International first broke in May 1998, the *Cincinnati Enquirer* got behind it big-time by running it in an eighteen-page special section. The story offered an investigative look at Chiquita's business practices, which, according to the reporter who wrote the story, left a lot to be desired.

The story accused Chiquita of spraying Costa Rican workers with dangerous pesticides, of setting up land trusts to hide secret investments in Honduras, and bribing Colombian officials. They were serious charges, which the reporter backed up with sources that offered minute details of the alleged wrongdoing.

Incredibly, none of the major news organizations picked up the story for distribution. Hoping to capitalize on publicity generated by the story, an anti-Chiquita group held a rally in Washington, D.C., but almost no one attended. To everyone's surprise, the newspaper's top banana story died a quick death.

Cincinnati Enquirer editors thought it was a dead issue until they heard from attorneys from Chiquita, who threatened to sue. Chiquita denied all the allegations made in the story and made charges of its own, namely, that the reporter had hacked into its computer system to steal confidential voice mails and other inter-office communications.

If true, it meant the story, true or false, had been compromised. It is one thing for a reporter to publish stolen information, but another thing entirely for a reporter to participate in the stealing of documents or recorded information considered privileged.

After conducting an investigation of its own, the *Cincinnati Enquirer*, which is owned by the Gannett media chain, fired the reporter, paid Chiquita a reported ten million dollars, and offered a public apology. In a front-page story that ran for three consecutive days, the *Cincinnati Enquirer* admitted that the voice-mail tapes had been taken illegally. The newspaper also published a page one acceptance of the apology from Chiquita, which won a huge victory without ever firing a legal shot.[1]

THE APOLOGY

"The representations, accusations, and conclusions [in the story] are untrue and created a false and misleading impression. . . ." In addition, publisher Harry Whipple said the voice-mail tapes had been gathered improperly, "in violation of the standards and practices of this newspaper."

NEWSSTAND CNN & TIME
NEWS MAGAZINE TRAPPED IN VALLEY OF DEATH

Following the corporate merger of CNN and Time-Warner, executives in both companies searched for ways to combine the efforts of the television news network with those of its magazines, especially *Entertainment Weekly* and *Time*.

First out of the chute was *NewsStand: CNN & Entertainment Weekly*. The CNN television show premiered without a hitch and quickly found a dedicated viewership. Encouraged by its success, the executives drew up plans for *NewsStand: CNN & Time*. For its premier show, producers chose an investigative feature they titled "Valley of Death."

Researched by CNN producers April Oliver and Jack Smith—and narrated by veteran television newsman Peter Arnett—the report alleged that during the Vietnam War, American Special Forces went on secret missions into Laos and used lethal sarin gas to kill American defectors.

If true, it was an astonishing story, for it stated that the American military not only used gas outlawed by the Geneva accords but also murdered American soldiers who had left their posts in opposition to the Vietnam War.

Unfortunately, when the story aired it became evident that the CNN news team did not have the evidence to back up its claims. What at first appeared to be the story of the decade quickly turned into the embarrassment of the century. After an in-house review of the story by well-known media attorney Floyd Abrams, CNN president Tom Johnson issued a retraction of the story and made an apology for the news network's mistake. Johnson announced that CNN producers Smith and Oliver had been fired, and that Arnett had been reprimanded. Said Johnson: "CNN's system of journalistic checks and balances, which has served CNN exceptionally well in the past, failed in this case."[2]

THE APOLOGY

"There is insufficient evidence that sarin or any other deadly gas was used," Tom Johnson said to television viewers in an apology that was broadcast repeatedly on CNN. "Furthermore, CNN cannot confirm that American defectors were targeted or at the camp as *NewsStand* reported."

MODERN LIBRARY
TOP 100 TAKES UNEXPECTED LITERARY ACID TRIP

From all appearances it was a great idea. It gave the marketing department something they could really sink their teeth into (marketing departments of publishing houses are notoriously hungry for meaty snacks, even if they are mostly bones).

Modern Library, the esteemed Random House division that turns out classic reprints by the bushel load, decided to convene a "board" of experts to choose the one hundred best novels in English of the twentieth century.

On the board were novelists William Styron and Gore Vidal; historians Daniel Boorstin, Shelby Foote, and Arthur Schlesinger Jr.; Modern Library board chairman Christopher Cerf, son of Random House founder Bennett Cerf; and biographer Edmund Morris. It was quite a gathering of the minds.

When the Top 100 list was released to the public, there was quite a clamor as newspapers and magazines examined the list, especially the Top 10, which included James Joyce (*Ulysses*) at number one, F. Scott Fitzgerald (*The Great Gatsby*) at number two, and James Joyce (*A Portrait of the Artist as a Young Man*), again, in the number-three position.

What Modern Library did not explain at the time was that more than half the books on the list were published by Modern Library.

When reporters dug even deeper, they discovered that the board members had not actually ranked the authors, listing them one though one hundred, but had merely listed the book they thought belonged on the list.

Once the list became a news item, there was nothing for Modern Library to do but to apologize—sort of.

THE APOLOGY

"The process is to some degree a scam, but it's a good scam," said board chairman Christopher Cerf.[3]

HELLO!
KEVIN COSTNER GETS THE LAST WORD

On March 8, 1997, *Hello!* magazine published an interview with actor Kevin Costner that quoted him as making unflattering remarks about his former wife, Cindy, and about ex-girlfriend Bridget Rooney, the mother of Costner's son, Liam.

In the article Costner was quoted as saying that Rooney had "tricked [him] into thinking she was using contraception when she wasn't." He was also quoted as saying the child had been "forced" on him. "'I'll try to help this child,'" continued the article, quoting Costner, "'but I'm afraid that he'll never mean the same to me as the others.'"

It was an interview the trade calls a "sizzler."

There was only one problem. Costner said he never gave the interview and never said any of the hurtful things attributed to him in the article. Outraged, he filed the first libel lawsuit of his career.

The lawsuit charged that *Hello!* had put Costner "in a false light in the public eye . . . portraying [him] as not properly dedicated to his profession . . . not a serious filmmaker, and more devoted to sport and pleasure than to his career."

Less than a month after the lawsuit was filed, *Hello!* printed a formal apology to Costner following an internal investigation.

THE APOLOGY

"We . . . fully accept that [Costner] never gave any such interview."[4]

JANET DAILEY
NOVELIST ROMANCED BY PLAGIARISM

For one of America's best-selling romance authors, the nightmare began innocently enough during an on-line computer chat with her readers. Janet Dailey, who has written nearly one hundred books over two decades, was asked about similarities between three of her books—*Notorious*, *Scrooge Wore Spurs*, and *Aspen Gold*—and books written by one of her literary rivals, Nora Roberts.

Subsequently, "fans" posted similar passages from both writers on a Web site.

Dailey admitted to copying Roberts's work.

Almost overnight, the incident became front-page news.

Roberts announced that she intended to file a copyright-infringement lawsuit against America's number-one romance novelist (Dailey's books have sold more than 200 million copies, while Roberts's books have sold about 50 million copies).

Dailey's lawyer told reporters that while his client had admitted copying Roberts's books, not all copying constituted copyright infringement. As legal technicalities about plagiarism were bandied about, Dailey did what any self-respecting romance heroine would do when confronted with the inescapable truth: She apologized.

The plagiarism occurred, she said, in the early 1990s while she was under professional and personal stress. Two of her brothers died of cancer and her husband, Bill, underwent surgery for lung cancer and then later had an aneurysm.

The stress was more than she could bear, she said, so she took the easy way out.

THE APOLOGY

"I do not excuse what I did. I can only apologize to Nora, whom I've considered a friend, and to my readers for any pain or embarrassment my conduct has caused. I also wish to apologize to the publishers of *Aspen Gold* and *Notorious*.

"It will never happen again. I'm embarrassed."[5]

ANDY ROONEY
JUST AN ACCIDENT WAITING TO HAPPEN

Over the years, *60 Minutes* curmudgeon Andy Rooney has offended his share of television viewers with his opinionated comments about the changing world around him. For the most part, he likes things the way they were.

Of course, he doesn't always confine his prickly barbs to the television show.

In a syndicated newspaper column published in September 1999, Rooney stirred up a firestorm of female protest when he suggested that most beautiful women in television news had been somewhat disfigured by plastic surgery.

"One of the most beautiful—OK THE most beautiful—women in television news had a job done on herself a few years ago and, while she doesn't look bad, she does not look the same or as good to me as when she had what must have seemed to her to be shortcomings," he wrote. "She looks as if she had been in a minor automobile accident."

Rooney didn't name the woman, but gossip columnists fanned the flame by trying to guess her identity. Some suggested it was Diane Sawyer, Rooney's former colleague on *60 Minutes*. Others were certain he was referring to Barbara Walters or Christiane Amanpour or Jane Pauley or Lesley Stahl or Connie Chung.

Under attack, Rooney staged a hasty retreat, proving with dazzling footwork that, contrary to conventional wisdom, elderly white men can jump with alacrity when backed into a corner.

THE APOLOGY

The uproar was much ado about nothing, Rooney said.

The woman he referred to in his newspaper column was a composite, he admitted: "I was writing metaphorically. I didn't have anybody really in mind."

Saying that he regretted ever writing the column, he bemoaned the exposure his ill-considered words brought him: "I didn't mean to call this much attention to myself."

Finally, he apologized to Diane Sawyer, who had received the most scrutiny from the media. "Diane is a good friend of mine and I like her a lot," said Rooney. "I think she's not only one of the great people in television, but she's one of the good people, too. She's as smart as she is beautiful."[6]

GERALDO RIVERA
TELEVISION SHOWMAN SNAPS AT GOLDEN GOOSE

The television career of Geraldo Rivera has been interesting, to say the least.

His two-hour exploration of Al Capone's empty vault, carried on live television, made him look foolish. His trashy daytime talk show that featured teen satanists and prostitutes made him look opportunistic. But his coverage of the O. J. Simpson trial and aftermath offered him an opportunity to blend his legal knowledge—he was a lawyer before becoming a television commentator—with his sense of showmanship.

Apparently, it was the latter talent that attracted the attention of NBC News, which offered him a $36 million contract to join its network news team as the host of a new show on CNBC called *Rivera Live*. Geraldo was attracted not just to the money, but to the respectability it offered.

Imagine everyone's surprise when the "new" Geraldo turned on his bosses with statements, published in *TV Guide*, that alleged that promos for his show didn't air during *Nightly News* because Tom Brokaw banned them.

Why would Brokaw ban Geraldo's promos?

According to Geraldo, it was because the news anchor knew Geraldo was "in the running for the center chair at the desk of the wise men." Not surprisingly, Brokaw declined to comment on Geraldo's allegations.

Not content with simply slapping the NBC Golden Goose about the beak, Geraldo went on a tear on the *Today Show* during an interview with conservative commentator Laura Ingraham. After Geraldo engaged in a shouting match with Ingraham on the air, cohost Katie Couric scolded him for not being impartial.

THE APOLOGY

Geraldo apologized to everyone involved.

To *Today Show* executive producer Jeff Zucker, he said, "I screwed up."

To NBC News, he apologized by issuing a written statement. "Tom Brokaw is a great newsman who does a terrific job, and the rivalry between us is grossly overstated." He went on to say that his ambition to become the "news anchor of the next millennium" was confined to his current job as host of *Rivera Live*.[7]

CHRIS MATTHEWS
CNBC NEWSMAN TOSSES BEANBALL

CNBC newsman Chris Matthews has a sterling reputation as a journalist. Sometimes even the best journalists misstep, however—especially when they are under the pressure of a deadline. Matthews's blunder occurred during the public hysteria over whether President Bill Clinton had groped Kathleen Willey in the Oval Office and then had tried to intimidate her into keeping quiet.

While interviewing Willey for his CNBC program *Hardball*, Matthews suggested that she had told him that a man named Cody Shearer had confronted her outside her Richmond home and tried to intimidate her. Willey would not confirm Matthews's allegations on the air.

Through his attorney, Shearer denied any involvement with Willey. A few days later, Matthews ran into Shearer, also a journalist, by coincidence at the Philadelphia Amtrak station. Shearer strongly disputed Matthews's claims and said he could produce receipts that would prove that he was in California the entire month in which the incident was alleged to have happened. Matthews found Shearer's denials credible.

To his credit, he apologized to Shearer without delay.

THE APOLOGY

Matthews made his apology during his program, *Hardball*, telling viewers he was sorry for the way he had handled the story: "I now regret not having spoken beforehand with [Shearer] before I mentioned his name on the air. I should never have brought his name up until we had vetted it."[8]

EXPRESS SUNDAY MAGAZINE
TOM AND NICOLE WIN WITH EYES WIDE OPEN

In an article titled "Cruising for Bruising . . . What's the Inside Story on Hollywood's Golden Couple," London's *Express Sunday Magazine* reported that Tom Cruise and Nicole Kidman had a marriage that was a hypocritical sham.

The newspaper magazine said the couple's marriage was a mere business arrangement, entered into by the couple on orders of the Church of Scientology, or as a cover-up for the homosexuality of one or both of them. Furthermore, the magazine stated, Cruise was impotent and sterile, and his public denial of that was untrue.

That was a bit more than Tom and Nicole wanted to hear, so they filed a lawsuit against the newspaper, charging the publication with libel. Cruise described the article as "vicious lies about me and my family."

In October 1998, the lawsuit was settled in London's High Court, with Cruise and Kidman receiving a reported six-figure payment from the newspaper. Cruise attended the court proceeding in order to hear the apology from the magazine.

Outside the courtroom, Cruise told reporters: "I really don't take a lot of pleasure being here today. This is the final recourse against those who have printed vicious lies about me and my family. I have to protect my family."

During the hearing, Cruise's attorney told the court that the article had caused his clients "grave personal distress." The proceedings had established the truth, he said: "They married solely because they loved each other, and their marriage is a close and happy one." As he left the court, Cruise signed autographs and posed on the steps for photographers.[9]

THE APOLOGY

In the courtroom, Patrick Moloney, attorney for the newspaper, said his clients wished to withdraw all the allegations the magazine made about Tom Cruise and Nicole Kidman:

"They wish, through me, to express their sincere apologies for the hurt and distress that they have caused."

TV GUIDE
MAGAZINE STANDS TALL FOR LUCILLE BALL

It all began with Walter Winchell, the popular radio commentator and newspaper columnist who dominated what we now call the tabloid news market. In the early to mid-1950s, the hottest news item in America was the Communist Party—and Congress's investigation of Hollywood writers, directors, and producers who had been targeted, usually by anonymous sources, as potential communists.

Without mentioning Lucille Ball by name, Winchell announced on his nationwide radio broadcast that "the most popular of all television stars has been confronted with her membership in the Communist Party."

Everyone knew he was talking about Lucille Ball, the costar of the television show *I Love Lucy*, which had premiered in 1951. Following up on Winchell's story was the *Los Angeles Herald Express* (now the *Los Angeles Herald-Examiner*), which sent a reporter to the CBS studio where Lucy was getting ready to film an episode of her show before a live audience.

Lucy's husband, Desi Arnaz, was outraged. He grabbed the reporter, who was carrying a camera and shook him by the neck, screaming at the top of his voice. Once Desi calmed down, the reporter told him the newspaper had a photostatic copy of an affidavit that proved that his wife had once registered as a Communist.

Desi called the reporter's editor and told her that his wife would be giving no interviews. He demanded that she call the reporter back to the newspaper. She did and the reporter left the studio, but by then Lucy was in hysterics.

Desi thought the crisis was over, but the newspaper printed the story anyway, under a headline in red ink: LUCILLE BALL A RED.

For a while it looked as if Lucy's career was over. There was concern that *I Love Lucy* sponsor Philip Morris might withdraw its sponsorship. Then there was fear that CBS Television would cancel the show.

Desi called the head of CBS, who told him that the network would stand behind Lucy. Then Desi called Rep. Donald Jackson of the House of Un-American Activities Committee and demanded that he hold a press conference and exonerate Lucy of any guilt. Jackson agreed to hold the press conference. Then Desi called a friendly reporter at the Associated Press to make sure the press conference was covered.

Lucille Ball was quickly cleared of any ties to the Communist Party—she was a redhead, for heaven's sake, not a Red—but the right-wing press continued its attacks against the actress. Westbrook Pegler, a well-known right-wing newspaper columnist whose column appeared in hundreds of newspapers, wrote that Lucy "had not come clean, but had to be tracked down and exposed."

After filming that week's episode of *I Love Lucy*, Desi and Lucy held a press conference at their ranch. It was then that Dan Jenkins of *TV Guide* rose to his feet and apologized for

THE APOLOGY

"I think we all owe Lucy an apology," Jenkins said.

the way Lucy had been treated by the news media.

After Jenkins spoke, everyone applauded, with the exceptions of Pegler and Winchell, who were not there. However, later that evening Winchell announced on his radio broadcast that Lucy had been completely cleared.

I Love Lucy remained the number-one show on television, but war veterans' groups contin-ued to protest against Lucy. The American Legion threatened to boycott Philip Morris cigarettes until they withdrew their sponsorship of the show.

The entire nightmare ended abruptly, the result of a single gesture by one man—President Dwight D. Eisenhower, who invited Lucy and Desi, and costars Vivian Vance and William Frawley, to dinner at the White House.[10]

CURSE OF THE DEAD ELVIS
NEWSPAPER EDITOR TANGLES WITH KING'S GHOST

Probably best known as the Magnolia State's solitary oasis of old-time liberalism and literary experimentation, Greenville, Mississippi, is a small town located on the banks of the Mississippi River, about eighty miles south of Memphis.

On that solemn day, August 14, 1977, when Elvis Presley crossed over the Great Spiritual Divide, Greenville's only newspaper, the *Delta Democrat-Times,* was under the editorship of Philip Carter, youngest son of legendary journalist Hodding Carter.

Philip was a proud and obedient son, but a reluctant editor. At the time the editorship was thrust upon him, he was living in New Orleans, where he published a weekly arts and entertainment tabloid. Putting out both publications required him to commute to New Orleans on a weekly basis.

The morning after Elvis's death, the *Delta Democrat-Times* published an editorial written by Philip that noted the passing of Mississippi's most famous native son. "As disapproving parents used to love to say, Elvis Presley was vulgar and common as dirt . . . ," began the editorial. It went on to credit Elvis with the invention of rock 'n' roll, something "so supremely vulgar that it swept the world."

To Philip's surprise—and ultimate horror—the newspaper was inundated with protests. When rumors circulated that there were plans afoot to bomb the editor's main street apartment, Philip packed up and left for New Orleans a few days early.

When he returned the following week, it was clear that an apology was in order.

To appease the indignant populace, Philip wrote a second editorial under the headline MORE ON ELVIS.

THE APOLOGY

"Speak no ill of the dead . . . Nothing that has appeared in this space in recent months has provoked such a stormy reaction as those few score well-intended words about the departed king of rock 'n' roll. What we meant was that Elvis Presley was 'vulgar' in the sense of one ancient meaning of that word as listed in our Webster's Dictionary: That meaning is, 'Of, or relating to, the common people'. . . Although a lot of people apparently didn't understand our intentions, we sincerely meant that as a wholly complimentary explanation of Elvis Presley's extraordinary appeal to millions."[11]

WEEKLY STANDARD
MEDIA MAGNATE FORCED TO EAT CROW

New Age oracle Deepak Chopra used to tell the story of the time he was lecturing before a large audience and a woman he had never seen before jumped to her feet and accused him of raping her. Stunned, Chopra asked when the supposed rape took place.

The woman replied that she wasn't sure of the exact date since it occurred in a previous life.

That's a funny story, all right, but not so funny was the 1997 story published by the *Weekly Standard* alleging that Chopra used the services of a San Francisco call girl on three occasions in 1991. The story also alleged instances of plagiarism by Chopra.

Outraged, Chopra filed a $35 million lawsuit against media mogul Rupert Murdoch, owner of the *Weekly Standard* and its sister publication, the *New York Post*, which also published the story.

When the prostitute who made the allegations was shown evidence that Chopra was in India at the time the supposed encounters took place, she recanted her statements and signed a sworn statement that she had mistaken Chopra for someone else and had, in fact, never met the man. Sorry about that little misunderstanding, she said.

Of course, it wasn't the apology of a prostitute that Chopra sought.

THE APOLOGY

In an unprecedented action, Rupert Murdoch published an apology in both the *Weekly Standard* and the *New York Post* retracting the story. Allegations about plagiarism and the use of a prostitute, said the apology, were "inappropriate and unjust."[12]

NORMAN MAILER

AUTHOR TAKES A STAB AT EXISTENTIAL REMORSE

Norman Mailer is one of the most influential writers of the twentieth century, at least in this writer's opinion. Even if his legacy were measured only by three books—*The Naked and the Dead*, *Armies of the Night*, and *The Executioner's Song*—his place in American literature would remain secure for years to come.

Of course, that's not to say that Mailer didn't have a few problems along the way.

Marriage is not an institution in which Mailer does his best work. It was on the evening of November 19, 1960—an occasion on which he announced his candidacy for mayor of New York—that his weaknesses in that area became apparent.

To celebrate Norman's candidacy, the Mailers gave a party that continued into the wee hours of the following morning. By 4:30 A.M. all of the guests had gone home. Mailer was spotted by neighbors out in the street chasing people and getting into fights, according to Carl Rollyson, author of the biography *The Lives of Norman Mailer*.

The following sequence of events is presented in Rollyson's book:

When Mailer returned to his apartment, he was greeted by his wife, Adele, who took one look at his black eye, bloodied face, and blood-stained bullfighter's shirt and made a disparaging remark about his condition.

Mailer removed a two-and-a-half-inch pen-knife from his pocket and stabbed Adele—once in the stomach and once in the back. One of the wounds was dangerously near her heart, but Adele survived the attack. Mailer was arrested.

A judge sent Mailer to a mental hospital for an evaluation, where he stayed for two weeks until he found a doctor who was prepared to declare him sane. When he returned to court, he was convicted of third-degree assault and given probation.

Not giving Mailer probation was Adele, who divorced him the following year.

The stabbing put Mailer on the spot.

It is difficult to have a successful career as a writer if there are doubts about one's sanity. In that sense, wearing the label of a wife knifer was preferable to being stamped crazy—and, for years after the incident, Mailer walked a very thin line between the two.

In an interview with Mailer published in January 1968, *Playboy* asked the writer about charges that he had a deep-seated hostility toward women.

In later years, Mailer condemned himself for the stabbing, saying that what he did was indefensible. In his own way, he apologized to everyone who had ever trusted him as a writer. He seemed to view the stabbing in biblical terms, as if it had been a battleground between good and evil. Interestingly, the one person he never apologized to, at least not publicly, was his ex-wife, Adele.

THE APOLOGY

"I think I've got as much anger against women as anyone I know, but I'm perfectly willing to let the defense rest right here—I don't give a damn—and, you know, I sometimes have as much hostility against women as I've got against men."

Then the magazine quoted a poem written by Mailer in which he equates the use of a knife on a woman with feelings of love for her. Didn't those lines, asked the magazine, boastfully exploit the stabbing of his wife? "I don't want to talk about the stabbing anymore," Mailer said. "Say the word eighteen times and it loses its force."[13]

60 MINUTES
TELEVISION NEWSMAGAZINE BEGS PARDON

On June 1, 1997, CBS Television's *60 Minutes* aired a segment titled "The Connection." The investigative piece was an edited-down version of a British-produced story about how the Cali drug cartel was smuggling heroin into Europe from Colombia.

There was no reason to doubt the accuracy of the report—it already had won awards for its reporting—but before airing it, *60 Minutes* producers reportedly interviewed the story's producer, Marc de Beaufort, and verified the plausibility of the story with the United States Drug Enforcement Administration.

Once the program aired, *60 Minutes* producers realized they had been duped. An independent investigation indicated that the show's producers had faked locations and used actors to play drug dealers.

60 Minutes had broadcast fiction and labeled it fact.

The task of going public with the details of the fraud fell into the lap of *60 Minutes* executive producer Don Hewitt, who had been with the news magazine since its inception, nearly thirty years ago.

In all that time, he had never been before a camera.

The fake segment's producer, de Beaufort, was unapologetic. He blamed a researcher for any false information contained in the piece. However, his employer, Carlton Communications, returned all the awards and all the fees collected for the sale of the piece.

THE APOLOGY

"We, you, and television viewers in fourteen other countries were taken," Hewitt said to viewers in his on-air apology. "To make amends, we felt obligated to lay it all out in detail and ask you to please accept our apology."

Hewitt said that none of the show's personnel would be reprimanded, but he admitted that the incident had made him less likely to use outside content in the future.[14]

LEONARD MALTIN
FILM CRITIC EATS HIS OWN WORDS (GAG!)

Leonard Maltin's reputation as a film critic is solid.

Imagine everyone's surprise when he was forced to *apologize* for a review he did of the film *Dusty and Sweets McGee*. It wasn't his comments about the film that got him into trouble. It was what he said about actor Billy Gray that brought him to his knees.

To those of you who do not remember Billy Gray, he played the role of the teenage son, Bud, on the popular 1960s sitcom *Father Knows Best*. He was a squeaky-clean kid who always seemed to agonize over what was right and wrong.

In his review of the movie, Maltin referred to a 1971 movie about Los Angeles heroin addicts, in which Gray had appeared. Maltin implied that Gray was a junkie when he did the movie. Gray, who was obviously offended by that implication, filed a lawsuit in Los Angeles Superior Court. Maltin settled the lawsuit out of court.

Looking chastened and somewhat embarrassed, Maltin appeared at a press conference at Hollywood's Roosevelt Hotel to tell an assembly of reporters, including a handful from the tabloids, who hung on his every word, that he was sorry about his comments about Billy Gray.

THE APOLOGY

"I did not mean to convey that Billy Gray was a heroin addict or pusher in my review of the film *Dusty and Sweets McGee*," Maltin said to reporters, then added that Gray had already accepted his personal apology. Ever the critic, Maltin said that he enjoyed watching Gray on reruns of *Father Knows Best*, and he wished the actor the best of luck in his career.[15]

NEW IDEA MAGAZINE

BRUCE AND DEMI NIBBLE ON AUSTRALIAN MAG

In the July 12, 1997, issue of *New Idea*, a women's magazine published in Australia, there was a feature story on Bruce Willis and Demi Moore. The headline read: "Demi's Bulimia Hell."

The story said that Demi's marriage was being destroyed by her alleged obsession with exercise and her eating disorder. Not taking kindly to that assessment of their marriage were Bruce and Demi, who promptly filed a lawsuit that charged that the magazine article was false and defamatory.

THE APOLOGY

In a full-page apology and retraction, *New Idea* magazine set the record straight:

"*New Idea* acknowledges that there was no foundation for any such suggestions. *New Idea* unconditionally withdraws any suggestion."[16]

Chapter 2

Movies and Television

GWYNETH PALTROW
HEART OF STONE ATTACKS BLOND INGENUE

After starring in *Emma* and *Shakespeare in Love*, which won her an Oscar, Gwyneth Paltrow must have thought guest-hosting *Saturday Night Live* would be a piece of cake. How tough could ninety minutes of live comedy possibly be?

Paltrow proved to be a real trooper.

In a sketch about a cable channel covering Bill Clinton's impeachment trial as if it were a Hollywood event, the blond actress acted out a parody of Sharon Stone arriving with her husband, Phil Bronstein.

The imitation Stone underwent a red-carpet interview, all the time hanging on to the arm of her husband, her responses alternating between vapid and giddy. At one point she looked at her imitation husband and said, "Isn't he creepy?"

As other stars were interviewed, Paltrow-as-Stone remained in the back-ground, mugging for the camera as if publicity were the true nectar of life. The skit was funny enough, but no one thought to tell the inexperienced Paltrow that it was generally frowned upon for an actress who had recently won an Oscar to poke fun at a more experienced actress who had gone home empty-handed from the same ceremony.

Seven months after the February 1999 *SNL* broadcast, Stone struck back. In an interview with *Movieline* magazine, Stone said she did not appreciate Paltrow's parody of her, especially the part about her husband.

"Gwyenth Paltrow is very young and lives in a rarefied air that's very thin," said Stone. "It's like she's not getting enough oxygen."

Stone went on to say that while she felt the younger actress has "a lot of talent," she considered her to be somewhat "naive."

THE APOLOGY

By the time Stone's comments were published, Paltrow had dyed her hair black for a new movie role and quietly disappeared from public view. The task of responding to Stone fell to her publicist, Stephen Huvane.

"Gwyneth doesn't write the skits on *SNL*," he said. "She was a performer. It wasn't anything personal."[17]

TORI SPELLING
THERE ARE NO VIRGINS IN THE MILE-HIGH CLUB

Tori Spelling just can't seem to make up her mind.

Is it better to be viewed as an eternal virgin, someone who is forever on the verge of stepping across the line (sort of a Mary Tyler Moore for the millennium)? Or is it better to be viewed as a hopelessly romantic slut, someone who is forever trying to step back across the line into celibacy?

There's yet another possibility—lesbianism. It's trendy, it's clean, it's less taxing physically than sex with males. So, what's a girl to do?

Going through life as the daughter of Aaron Spelling, one of the entertainment industry's richest tycoons, certainly hasn't helped her make up her mind. Each week she has dinner with her father, a man who calls everyone, male or female, babe!

How confusing it must be for a girl who doesn't know who she is to be in the presence of an intimidating father who knows *exactly* who everyone in the entertainment industry is at all times. If, for some reason, they don't know who they are, he will tell them in quick order, *Yeah, babe, you got it!*

When Tori was asked by *Playboy* magazine in early 1998 to do an interview for its "20 Questions" feature, she must have perceived the request as a sign that fate was coming down squarely on the side of her assuming the role of a hopelessly romantic fallen woman. Why else would *Playboy* be interested in her?

In the interview, *Playboy* wasted no time getting to the meat of the matter. Tori was asked who she thought had the best cleavage in Hollywood. She chose Madonna, but then said Pamela Anderson Lee had some "pretty nice" breasts.

Playboy asked why being a stripper ranked at the top of many women's fantasies. Tori answered that she thought it was because women had been conditioned to feel like they had to look sexy for men. She said that if she could get away with it without being recognized, she would definitely like to give stripping a whirl.

Then *Playboy* asked if there was anything about herself that would shock her parents. To the interviewer's surprise, Tori dropped a bombshell. She confessed that she once had sex in the bathroom of an airplane while traveling to Europe with her boyfriend.

"We figured that people must do it all the time," she said. "It was a small stall, though, so it was hard to move around. It's not like it's very sexy or romantic, but it gets the job done. I had planned to do it all along, so I was prepared and wore a long skirt."

THE APOLOGY

Almost one year after her confession to *Playboy*, Tori Spelling was asked by *US* magazine if she had any regrets. Did she ever!

Tori said her admission of airborne sex had been a huge mistake.

"Oh, gosh, I got so much flak for that, oh, my God," she said. "It was this long flight on one of those double-decker planes. I don't know. I'd like to sweep it under the rug. I'd like to forget all about it, including the guy."[18]

RILEY WESTON
AGE BIAS FINDS NEW ADVOCATE

For ten years Kimberlee Kramer played bit parts on television and in the movies. Always she was cast as one of the teenagers in the crowd. When she turned thirty, she looked back over her decade-long career with dismay. Petite, with a youthful face, she was still playing the role of an eighteen-year-old nobody—and getting nowhere fast.

In 1996, she decided to do something about that. She changed her name to Riley Weston, wrote up a new résumé that contained none of her previous acting experience, and chopped twelve years off her age.

When pretty, doe-eyed Riley Weston showed up at the offices of WB Network's *Felicity*, it was to apply for a job as an eighteen-year-old writer. The executives who interviewed her, all of whom were her actual age, were impressed that a woman that age could be so knowledgeable about the industry. They hired her as quick as you could say, "Teen Fever."

Almost overnight, Wiley became a celebrity. *Entertainment Weekly* named her as one of the one hundred most creative people in show business and wrote a glowing profile about her. *Felicity* producers were so impressed with one of her scripts that they gave her a small role in the episode that she wrote.

Impressed by her rapid rise to celebrity status, Disney's Touchstone Television offered her a $50,000 two-year writing contract. Unfortunately, hell hath no fury like a friend who has been scorned by the bitch goddess of success. Within a week of the announced Disney deal, an anonymous caller blew the whistle on the eighteen-year-old wonder child: Riley Weston was a fraud.

THE APOLOGY

Once she knew the story of her deception was going to become public knowledge, Riley Weston apologized to the cast of *Felicity*. She later told *Newsweek*, "Every day I wanted to tell them, (but) every day the show got hotter, every day it got harder."

Interviewed by *Entertainment Tonight*, she again apologized for misrepresenting her age, saying that she did it only to get work. Later, in a prepared statement, she said: "The current situation over my age was never a purposeful deception to advance my career as a writer. I could not be one age in the acting world and another in the writing world, so I chose to maintain the ruse. In a business fraught with age bias, I did what I felt I had to do to succeed."

TITANIC
STUDIO EXECUTIVE TRIES TO SET THINGS RIGHT

Hollywood's 1997 film *Titanic* was a massive hit.

In part, the Oscar-winning film owed its success to startling special effects and its sweeping vision of the sinking of the world's grandest ship. If the dialogue in the film was at times hyperbolic, that was fine with moviegoers, who realized they were watching a fictionalized rendering of a historical event.

Unfortunately, the filmmakers displayed occasional lapses in good judgment, such as when they used the names of actual living persons and attributed words and actions to them in an effort to make the script more interesting.

There is one segment in the film where First Officer William Murdock, the only Scottish officer aboard the ship, is depicted as a coward and murderer. In the film, he murders two passengers as they try to get into a lifeboat and then shoots himself dead.

Don't tell that to the residents of Dalbeattie, Scotland, Murdock's hometown, where he is regarded as a hero and commemorated by a plaque in the town hall. Dalbeattie residents let it be known that they were outraged by the film's treatment of their hero.

The task of apologizing fell to Scott Neeson, the executive vice president of 20th Century Fox, who traveled to Scotland on the eighty-seventh anniversary of the disaster.

During his April 1998 visit, Neeson apologized to Murdock's family for the "distress" caused by the film. He presented Murdock's old school with a check for five thousand pounds and an engraved plaque. In addition, he apologized to Murdock's eighty-year-old nephew, Scott Murdock, and presented him with a mounted dinner plate from the set of the film.

Scott Murdock accepted Neeson's apology. "I am very pleased that they have admitted their error. I don't think I can forget, but today certainly makes it easier to forgive."[19]

> ## THE APOLOGY
>
> "I am sorry we have caused you and your family so much distress," Neeson said to Scott Murdock. "Dalbeattie has every right to be proud of him. It was never intended to portray him as a coward. He saved a number of lives that night and has always been a hero, quite rightly. He did as much as he could and more than any other officer, apparently, to save lives, and I think that was portrayed in the film. Unfortunately, it was the other aspects that caused the offense."

DAVID DUCHOVNY
THE MEDIA MADE HIM DO IT

No one seems to know what David Duchovny was like before the popular television series *The X Files* made him into a star, so no one is certain if he has been changed for the worse by success. But everyone knows what he is like today.

Let's just say that the actor has a tendency to put his foot in his mouth, a condition that has been exacerbated, no doubt, by his loathing of the media, which has never been hesitant to report his reflections, no matter how strange.

In an interview that was published in the May 1999 issue of *Esquire*, Duchovny demonstrated once again why he has earned his reputation.

"I always feel, when somebody calls you a star, it's like they're saying 'fag.'" He said. "You know what I hear when somebody says 'star'? I hear 'pussy.' I don't know why." He explained that it might be because of the perks that celebrities are afforded. "You're getting great service, sure, but in the end they're thinking 'pussy.' I know they are. They're thinking, 'He couldn't take it if he had to sit in coach.'"

Duchovny's use of the word "fag" brought an immediate response from the Gay and Lesbian Alliance Against Defamation (GLAAD). Said a spokesperson: "Mr. Duchovny's juvenile remarks stand in sharp contrast to some very clever, interesting, and diverse roles we've seen him play in the last several years, and we are disappointed."

THE APOLOGY

David Duchovny wasted no time setting the record straight.

After learning of GLAAD's protest, the actor called the organization and apologized for his choice of words. A spokesman for the group told the *New York Daily News* that Duchovny said he had always been supportive of his gay friends and "how he wishes he had used a different negative word."

MATT GROENING
BART SIMPSON CREATOR LEARNS FOR HIMSELF

Exactly what Bart Simpson was meant to be in the beginning is known only to his creator, Matt Groening, but certainly as the cartoon figure developed into a prime-time television hit on *The Simpsons*, he assumed the role of America's first animated antihero.

Bart's irreverent antics inspired school-age children by the millions to adopt his personality as their own. The cartoon character's snappy rejoinders became the language of choice for ten-year-olds across the country:

"Ay, caramba!"

"Don't have a cow, man."

"I didn't do it. Nobody saw me do it. Can't prove anything."

The final straw for creator Groening came in 1997 when Children Now and the Henry J. Kaiser Family Foundation conducted a survey of children ages ten to seventeen to find out whom they most admired on television.

To everyone's surprise, Bart Simpson tied with *Home Improvement*'s Tim Allen for third place, with Michael Jordan and Will Smith in the one and two spots. Faced with such evidence, what's a cartoon creator to do?

Matt Groening pondered the results of that survey for almost two years.

Obviously, he needed to say something about his creation becoming a bad role model for kids. But what? One possibility was to allow Bart to speak for him: "I didn't do it. Nobody saw me do it. Can't prove anything." Of course, he *did* do it and everyone saw him do it. Groening opted for the unvarnished truth.

THE APOLOGY

"I now have a seven-year-old boy and a nine-year-old boy, so all I can say is I apologize."[20]

MELISSA JOAN HART
TV'S SABRINA FLAUNTS HER FEMININE MAGIC

First, she played a precocious teenager on Nickelodeon's *Clarissa Explains It All.* Then she landed a starring role in ABC Television's *Sabrina, the Teenage Witch.* Both roles called for her to project squeaky-clean images, veritable visions of what producers considered to be the ideal teenager.

For Melissa Joan Hart, that role became increasingly difficult to maintain off screen, especially when she turned twenty-one. By 1999, the twenty-three-year-old actress felt the need to exert her grown-up sexuality—not as Sabrina the witch but as Melissa Joan Hart, woman in waiting.

To the absolute horror of the publisher of Archie Comics, which owns the Sabrina character, Hart appeared in a series of sexy magazine covers, beginning with *Movieline* and *Bikini,* and ending with *Maxim,* which photographed her wearing panties and little else. The accompanying article in *Maxim* presented her in bed wearing a g-string, with the edge of the sheet covering her breasts. Another photo showed her in bikini-style underwear with her bra unfastened.

In the article, she answered questions about where she liked to be kissed (on her neck) and whether she could drink most guys under the table (no, but she confessed to downing twelve tequila shots in two hours on her twenty-first birthday).

Archie Comics publisher Michael Silberkleit went ballistic. He fired off a fax to Viacom, which had licensed the Sabrina character, and demanded that Hart apologize for damaging Sabrina's reputation. Said Silberkleit: "If Ms. Hart wants to change her image, she must wait until after her contract with Viacom expires and refrain from associating our Sabrina the Teenage Witch character with her personal endorsement of binge drinking, participation in pornography, and discussion about sex."

THE APOLOGY

"I'm not trying to change my image. . . . I'm not doing this for any kind of shock value, or to show that I can do this. I'm just trying to have fun, more than anything. . . . I do have to be careful. I still have a job, I still have fans, and my family and my mom have a lot of trust in me that I'm not going to disappointment them. My little brothers and sisters look up to me, so that keeps me in line. My little siblings are kind of like a small portion of my audience."[21]

CHER
IT WAS LETTERMAN'S WORST MOMENT (HE SAYS)

For years, producers of David Letterman's late-night show asked Cher to be a guest on the show. She always said no. Then one day they happened to ask at a time when the entertainer had an unpaid hotel bill of nearly $30,000.

Cher said she would do the show if they paid her hotel bill.

Letterman's producers said no, then, according to Cher in her book *The First Time*, they changed their minds and paid the bill. During a preshow conversation with Cher, one of the staff members asked her what she had against the talk-show host.

Cher said she thought he was an "asshole."

Later, during the actual show, Letterman asked Cher why she had never done his show. Cher stared at Letterman, and he stared back. She realized that the producer had told him what she had said. Both knew she couldn't possibly tell the truth.

"I was squirming," Cher said. "I really didn't mean to say it. I thought I was going to say something different. But then I looked at him smirking at me, and suddenly the words just jumped out of my mouth: 'Because I thought you were an asshole!'"

Cher's answer was bleeped by censors, but it was easy enough to read her lips.

Letterman laughed, but his comments about the incident (it was in the news for weeks and was relived repeatedly by the talk-show host himself during subsequent shows) indicated that, at some deeper, personal level, he had been hurt by her honesty.

When *People* magazine asked Letterman to describe the worst thing that ever happened to him, he readily answered that it was Cher calling him an asshole.

In an instant, Cher learned by accident what most of Letterman's female guests have yet to figure out: The talk-show host has different standards for male and female guests. He knows that he can push male guests only so far with his caustic humor before it erupts into a shoving match. Female guests, he has concluded, will take more heat.

Cher showed the entire world that the best way to put Letterman in his place is to go on the offensive. Calling him an asshole in front of the studio audience was tantamount to tossing a bucket of cold water on him.

Cher later apologized.

THE APOLOGY

"I wasn't trying to be mean-spirited. I was kind of playing with him. The truth is I liked him in spite of himself. Then he wrote me a really funny note, and we got to be kind of friends. Not close friends, though, because he never exhales." [22]

CHRISTIAN SLATER
MOVIE ACTOR SLIPS OVER THE EDGE, CRAWLS BACK

By August 1997, Christian Slater was on a roll.

Sure, he had experienced some legal problems (in 1994 he was detained by New York police after a pistol was found in his luggage at JFK Airport) and some personal problems (his girlfriend sued him for palimony), but he had a string of successful movies under his belt and life had never looked sweeter.

The nightmare began that August when he went to a Los Angeles apartment to party with a few friends. Present at the apartment were Marlon Brando's daughter Petra and her date, a man named Jacques, and their mutual friend Michelle with whom Slater already was acquainted.

Once Slater began drinking and snorting cocaine the party got a little crazy, according to police, who were called to intervene. The actor doesn't remember much of what happened that evening, but police told him he tried to jump off the balcony, attacked Michelle and punched her in the face, bit Jacques on the chest when he tried to help the woman, kicked a janitor in the stomach, and tried to seize a police officer's gun.

On January 14, 1998, the day after he attended the premiere for his movie *Hard Rain,* in which he costarred with Minnie Driver and Morgan Freeman, he was cuffed and taken off to jail, where he was sentenced to a term of ninety days.

Because he was so cooperative at the jail—his eagerness to wash patrol cars was well publicized—he was released after serving only sixty days. What he found when he walked outside was a phalanx of reporters, all of whom wanted answers.

"What the hell were you thinking?" asked a writer for *Rolling Stone* magazine.

"Well, where do I begin?" Slater answered. "I was born. The rest has all unfolded." He went on to explain that his troubles have all been the result of doing things his way and not God's way. "God's way is anything that starts out hard and gets easier. My way is things that start out easy and get more difficult."

The magazine writer asked him if he was prepared to take responsibility for what happened that day in the apartment.

THE APOLOGY

"I take full ownership of the incident," he said, coming as close as he ever would to an outright apology. "I haven't shown any great character doing drugs and alcohol. The cat's out of the bag on me, okay? I'm insane. No doubt about it. Crystal clear. I can't lie about it. I lie, I die. It's over."[23]

CALISTA FLOCKHART
ALLY McBEAL STAR SLAMS HER BREASTS

In the beginning, viewers and critics were so taken with the quirky Fox Television series *Ally McBeal* that they sort of overlooked its star, Calista Flockhart. As the series grew in popularity, Flockhart found herself in the crosshairs of public scrutiny:

Why is she so tiny?

Does she have sex on a regular basis?

Is she so tiny because she has an eating disorder?

Who's her boyfriend, anyway?

Will production have to be stopped because of her eating disorder?

And so on . . .

Those questions kept coming up so often in interviews that Flockhart stopped doing interviews—or at least started canceling those she thought would leave her in a defensive position about her weight. Of course, that only stoked the bonfires of media scrutiny and led to speculation that she was canceling interviews because of her supposed eating disorder. Through-out it all, Flockhart wondered if she was being a lousy role model for other women.

Of course, being the hypersensitive person that she is, she blamed herself. After weeks of jousting with the media—on *Late Night with David Letterman* she suggested that the news media should kiss her "bony ass"—she did a very *Ally McBeal*-esque turnaround. She apologized—not for anything she had done, but, rather, for being the person that she is.

THE APOLOGY

"If I had big boobs, none of this would have happened."

Later, she added: "I have to be who I am. I can't go out and gain weight . . . in order to be a better role model."[24]

ROZ KELLY
PINKY PULLS A BOO-BOO

Fans of the popular 1970s and early-1980s television series *Happy Days* remember Roz Kelly as Pinky Tuscadero, Fonzie's high-spirited, biker girlfriend. Beneath Pinky's crusty, tough-talking exterior was a heart of gold.

Pinky would do anything for the Fonz.

When the show went off the air in 1984, Kelly disappeared, too, except in syndication, where *Happy Days* reruns kept the actress suspended in time—always youthful, always attractive, always at Fonzie's side.

In early 1999, that image of Pinky experienced a rude awakening when Kelly was arrested for going on a shooting rampage with a shotgun. Witnesses told police that the former actress, then fifty-seven years of age, bolted from her North Hollywood home after being awakened by a noisy car alarm.

Shooting from the hip, say police, she pumped shotgun pellets into two cars owned by her neighbors—an Acura and a Mercury Topaz—and then went to the home of one of the car owners, broke out a window, and fired a blast from her Winchester into the living room. Kelly was arrested and charged with three felony firearms counts.

After initially pleading not guilty to the charges, Kelly changed her plea as part of a deal worked out with prosecutors. She received a three-year prison sentence, which was later reduced to probation by the judge, following a ninety-day psychiatric exam.

THE APOLOGY

Kelly apologized for the incident, saying that she had simply "snapped" after the car alarm kept going off and keeping her awake.

"I walked out the door of my home, aimed the shotgun at the car, and started shooting from the hip like there was no tomorrow," she said. "I never meant to become Annie Oakley and shoot up the town—I just wanted to escape from the pain."[25]

HUGH GRANT
WHAT WAS THE MAN THINKING?

In 1995, Hugh Grant was carrying around a certain amount of fame, the result of his role in the movie *Four Weddings and a Funeral*, in which he costarred with Andie MacDowell. But it was his girlfriend, supermodel Elizabeth Hurley, who attracted most of the media attention.

Imagine everyone's surprise when Grant was arrested by Los Angeles police on June 27, 1995, and charged with receiving oral sex from a Hollywood prostitute in his car. Both Grant and the prostitute, Divine Brown, were taken off to jail and booked.

Grant was charged with lewd conduct involving a prostitute.

When the news media got wind of Grant's arrest, reporters were speechless. They weren't shocked that a Hollywood actor had been busted on sex charges—it happens all the time—rather they were stunned that a man who was dating one of the most beautiful women in the world would resort to the services of a prostitute who was . . . well, not one of the most beautiful women in the world.

The story made headlines worldwide.

Within hours of his arrest, Grant issued a statement that acknowledged that his actions were "completely insane." He apologized to the public, to his friends, to everyone he worked with, and, of course, to Elizabeth Hurley.

As the story continued, day after day for two weeks, Grant decided he needed to make a more public apology. For that, he chose *The Tonight Show*, hosted by Jay Leno.

THE APOLOGY

When Grant walked out on stage and took a seat next to Leno's desk, the talk show host waited until the applause died down, then uttered the line that best expressed public interest in the incident: *"What the hell were you thinking?"*

Looking nervous and ill at ease, Grant was apologetic about the incident.

"I did a bad thing," he said, adding, "I keep reading new psychological theories that I was under pressure, I was overtired, I was lonely, I fell down the stairs as a child. That would be bollocks to hide behind that. You know in life what is a good thing and what is a bad thing. I did a bad thing and there you have it."[26]

DAVID SPADE
IT AIN'T EASY BEING THE LITTLE GUY

For most of his television career, David Spade has played characters whose sexuality has always been somewhat ambiguous, though there has never been any overt suggestion that the characters are anything but heterosexual.

Therein lies the mother lode for Spade's laughs.

Perhaps none of the characters Spade has played has a more ambiguous sexuality than Dennis Finch, the flighty-but-devious receptionist on NBC TV's *Just Shoot Me.*

In a recent *Playboy* interview, Spade criticized *Just Shoot Me* producers for the way in which they had worked to keep his character in that all-too-familiar box. "Sometimes they try to fag me up and I have to put my foot down," he said. "[My character] has all these fruity little traits that come out every week, and they try to whiz them past me. . . . [When] I get too faggy, they have me make out with a chick."

Those comments did not go over too well with members of the Gay and Lesbian Alliance Against Defamation (GLAAD), who promptly attacked the comedian for his remarks, which they saw as belittling to homosexuals.

Backed into a corner, Spade apologized for his comments through his publicist. The apology was not accepted by GLAAD.

"How can you consider using derogatory, hurtful rhetoric as 'good-natured'?" said a spokesman. "He wouldn't good-naturedly use racial or ethnic slurs."[27]

THE APOLOGY

"He was just trying to be a comedian, and everything he said was in good nature, and he's sorry if he offended anyone with his comments," said Spade's publicist.

RENE RUSSO
A FLASH IS WORTH A THOUSAND WORDS

I t's not easy going from supermodel to working actress—just ask Cindy Crawford or Claudia Schiffer—but Rene Russo managed to pull it off with grace and good humor.

Russo had a good run as a model during the 1970s, frequently appearing on the covers of *Vogue* and *Cosmopolitan*, but when she found herself, at the age of thirty-one, posing with a pillow on her stomach for a pregnancy catalog, she realized it was time to quit.

Russo's big break in movies occurred when she landed a supporting role as Tom Berenger's girlfriend in the movie *Major League*. A string of movies followed, including *Lethal Weapon 3*, *Get Shorty*, and *Outbreak*.

By the time she got the role playing opposite Pierce Brosnan in *The Thomas Crown Affair*, she had successfully exchanged her identity as a model for one of a serious actress. There was only one aspect of *The Thomas Crown Affair* that bothered her— the nudity that the script called for. Russo prayed for guidance on whether to do it.

"I don't know where in the Bible it says, 'Don't be nude in a motion picture,'" she told *Los Angeles* magazine. "In some of the most beautiful paintings in the Vatican, people are in the nude."

Evidently, Russo felt she got a thumbs-up from the Lord, for she agreed to do the nude scenes required in the script. Director John McTiernan knew she was uncomfortable with it, so he did everything he could to make it easier for her.

"Even though she's a model, Rene doesn't know she's gorgeous," McTiernan told the *New York Post*. "And she doesn't have an augmented body, by the way. Inside she doesn't know how pretty she is."

One of the scenes called for her to wear a transparent dress.

"She was so scared that she came to the set in a Michelin Man quilted coat," says McTiernan. "She looked like a GE refrigerator." To make her feel more secure, McTiernan cleared out the set, sending the crew members outside in the cold.

THE APOLOGY

"After the scene was over," says McTiernan, "Rene goes out there— and there are a hundred guys waiting in the cold—and by way of an apology, she stands at the top of the stairs and throws open the coat. It was a lovely gesture, and it took all the tension out."[28]

Chapter 3

Crime and
Punishment

AMY FISHER
"LONG ISLAND LOLITA" TAKES A HIKE

As a news story, it defined tabloid journalism in the early 1990s:

Sixteen-year-old student and part-time escort (Amy Fisher) has affair with middle-aged man (Joey Buttafuoco) and, while in a jealous rage, confronts the man's wife (Mary Jo) and pumps hot lead into her head.

It was a shocking story in many respects.

For starters, people didn't know whether to be more shocked over the affair or over the fact that the pretty teen worked part-time for an escort agency. Then there was the husband, Joey: *What was he thinking?* And the wife, of course, who was the unwitting victim in all of this.

What kind of people were these, anyway?

Several made-for-television movies, numerous books, and thousands of hours of television coverage attempted to answer that question. For a time, it seemed all of America was obsessed with the teen the tabloids were calling the "Long Island Lolita."

Not so baffled was the court system.

Fisher was sentenced to five to fifteen years in prison after pleading guilty to the crime. Joey Buttafuoco served six months in jail for statutory rape. And the victim . . . well, Mary Jo Buttafuoco, who still carries the bullet in her neck, has made a miraculous recovery from her injuries, though she still suffers from lingering nerve damage.

After seven years in prison, Amy Fisher succeeded in obtaining a hearing to determine if there was cause for a reduction in her prison sentence. Seated in the courtroom was Mary Jo Buttafuoco. She was there to hear an apology.

THE APOLOGY

From the witness stand, Fisher gazed at Mrs. Buttafuoco and spoke directly to her. "What happened to you, it wasn't your fault . . . it wasn't my father's fault," she said. "It was my fault, and I'm sorry."

Later, as she was led from the courtroom by guards, she walked past Mrs. Buttafuoco. They brushed fingers, and the younger woman, appearing to hold back tears, mouthed, "I'm sorry."

Outside the court-room, reporters asked Mrs. Buttafuoco how she felt about the apology. "Through faith in God I am able to forgive," she said. "It did not come easily or quickly."

In early May 1999, Fisher walked out of prison a free woman.[29]

LORENA BOBBITT
ON THE CUTTING EDGE OF CONTRITION CHIC

Without warning, Lorena Bobbitt crept upon her sleeping husband and whacked off his penis with a butcher knife. Then, still clutching her significant other's severed organ, she ran out of the house into the night. For some reason, she felt compelled to toss her prized trophy onto a grassy knoll beside a well-traveled road.

It all seemed to make sense to her at the time.

Luckily for her husband, police located the missing member and gingerly transported it to a hospital, where surgeons reattached it in a timely manner. Subsequently, while pursuing a short-lived career as a porn actor, the husband claimed his remodeled equipment worked good as new.

Not so lucky was Lorena, who went on trial for the headline-friendly attack.

THE APOLOGY

"My feelings . . . were all mixed up and I couldn't really explain," Lorena testified during her trial. "I couldn't stop. Couldn't help myself. I had to do it, see. I had this . . . I was overwhelmed by this . . . this . . . this . . . this irresistible impulse."[30]

HEIDI FLEISS
YOU CAN'T KEEP A GOOD GIRL DOWN

When she was arrested in 1993 on charges of pandering, Heidi Fleiss made headlines around the world. It's not that prostitution was such a major news story. It's *where* she did it—Hollywood—and the fact that her clients were movie stars and studio executives, that sent the news media into overdrive.

Fleiss's black book was rumored to bulge with the names of actors and studio moguls who were willing to pay her $1,500-a-night fee for sexual partners. Fleiss, who was labeled *the* Hollywood Madam, didn't turn tricks herself, but during her trial it became evident that her supermodel-type "girls" were worth every penny she charged. One of the biggest names in her black book, Charlie Sheen, testified at her trial that he spent over fifty thousand dollars on Fleiss's hookers.

Fleiss was convicted on the state's charges of pandering, but that conviction was later overturned on grounds of juror misconduct. Subsequently, she was tried in federal court on charges of tax evasion and money laundering.

Before going to prison, she opened a clothing store called Heidi's Wear, where she worked until they took her away. Upon her release from prison in September 1999, Fleiss filed for bankruptcy. She included debts of more than $269,000, $115,000 of which was owed to her lawyers.

On the Web site she created to sell products from her clothing store, she announced that she was back in business. Well, sort of. "I am out of prison and ready to autograph your T-shirts, so place your order now," she said. But below that message was this intriguing one: "Coming Soon: Adult web Sight [sic] that promises to be the ultimate sexual experience!"[31]

THE APOLOGY

At her trial in federal court, Fleiss made a tearful appeal to the judge.

"I am a different person now," she said. "I made terrible choices and mistakes."

Fleiss's attorney told the judge that his client was the victim of a sexist justice system that prosecuted madams but not their johns.

The judge seemed moved by both arguments.

"I believe you will be a positive role model for other young people and other women who could benefit from the experiences you've had," the judge told Fleiss. Then he sentenced her to thirty-seven months in a federal prison.

BETTIE PAGE
BABY DOES A BAD, BAD THING

Often called the most photographed model in history, Bettie Page appeared in hundreds of cheesecake magazines during the 1950s, earning her the unofficial title of America's favorite pin-up queen.

At the time, some called her a bad girl. Her bondage photographs were so notorious that she was called before a congressional subcommittee, ostensibly to answer questions about the pornography industry, though some cynics said the congressmen only wanted an excuse to meet Page in person.

All that attention frightened Page, who was not so much a bad girl as she was a naive Tennessee girl who liked to walk around naked. In 1957, at the height of her career, she walked away from it all and simply disappeared.

With time, she became a legend. As America's prototype Bad Girl, she was emulated in later years by rock singer Madonna, who copied her style down to the same lingerie-and-bondage imagery—and more recently grunge rocker Courtney Love.

Page did not resurface until the late 1970s.

After stabbing her elderly landlords for no apparent reason, she was committed to a California mental health treatment center after a judge ruled her not guilty by reason of insanity. She was released two years later on the condition that she continue to receive treatment as an outpatient.

In 1982, the state placed Page in the home of Leonie Haddad, a widow in her sixties who took in boarders to help make ends meet. On the morning of June 12, 1982, Haddad awoke to find Page straddling her in bed. In the moonlight she could see a foot-long knife in Page's hand.

"Don't scream," Page said. "God has inspired me to kill you."

Haddad was stabbed four times in the chest and eight times in her hand, which she had raised to protect herself, but she managed to survive the attack.

Page was charged with attempted murder. Since Page had been declared insane by state psychiatrists, the judge ordered her committed to the state mental hospital for a term of ten years. Once again, Page disappeared from public view.

After Bettie Page's trial, Haddad filed a lawsuit against the state hospital. It was settled out of court for a reported seventy thousand dollars. Just as life seemed to be getting back to normal for the elderly widow, she received a letter in the mail from Page.

America's pin-up queen wanted to apologize.

THE APOLOGY

"She told me, 'I was sorry for what I did to you. Regret it. Want to visit you one day,'" said Haddad, who immediately called her lawyer.
"I told him, don't let her write me again."[32]

Page was eventually diagnosed as schizophrenic and prescribed drug therapy. After more than a decade in a mental hospital, she was released in 1992, only to discover that she had become, during her long absence, a cult figure, an American pop-culture icon.

JUSTIN VOLPE

BLUE WALL OF SILENCE TOPPLES ONTO NEW YORK COP

It was one of the most publicized cases of police brutality in New York history.

It began with the 1997 arrest of a Haitian immigrant named Abner Louima, who was taken into a station-house rest room by New York police officers and beaten and sodomized. The case might never have come to public attention had the hospital officials who treated Louima not encouraged him to seek the services of an attorney.

After an internal investigation—during which the infamous "blue wall of silence" at first protected the police officers responsible for Louima's injuries, then backed away when details of the perverse nature of the crime came to light—five police officers, including Justin Volpe, were arrested and charged with first-degree assault and aggravated sexual assault.

Before the assault took place, Volpe borrowed a pair of gloves from a fellow police officer. When he returned them, they were covered in blood. That police officer subsequently testified against him.

Volpe eventually pleaded guilty to the assault and got thirty years from a judge, who said, "Short of intentional murder, one cannot imagine so barbarous an act."

THE APOLOGY

Justin Volpe's first apology went to the police officer from whom he borrowed the gloves he used in the assault. Upon returning them covered in blood, he said, "Sorry about the gloves, man."

The second apology came from Volpe's father, Robert Volpe, a retired police detective. Volpe—the devoted father, the proud cop—seemed to struggle to find the right words: "People have breaking points. People snap."

The final apology came from Justin Volpe, who issued it in the courtroom, shortly before the judge imposed the sentence:

"I am extremely sorry for my crime. I will go to prison twenty-seven years old and come out in a coffin."[33]

BRAD PITT'S VOODOO FAN
WOMAN BREAKS INTO STAR'S HOUSE WITH DOLL

After spending ten hours in Brad Pitt's Los Feliz, California, home, nineteen-year-old Athena Rolando was apprehended by police in his bedroom, where she allegedly had changed into the star's clothes. Pitt was not home at the time.

She was charged with entering or remaining illegally in a dwelling and illegally entering property with intent to injure property rights. Pitt's attorneys obtained a temporary restraining order that barred her from contacting the star or coming within one hundred yards of him.

Pitt's attorneys contended in court documents that Rolando was no stranger to the star and on previous occasions had left "menacing and bizarre letters" at the front gate of his home.

Rolando pleaded no contest to the charges and was sentenced to probation. In addition, the court barred the woman from contacting or getting within one hundred yards of Pitt for three years.

THE APOLOGY

Rolando's first apology was a letter she sent to Pitt before she was caught inside his house. According to court documents, the letter said she had confessed to putting a "chant" on Pitt and former girlfriend Gwyneth Paltrow three years earlier. "I was young and selfish," she said in the letter. "I am sorry. . . . I didn't think it would work, and your eyes have haunted me since then."

Rolando's second apology came after her court appearance. Speaking to reporters outside the courtroom, she said she had entered Pitt's house simply to give him a "beautiful" voodoo doll. "It's a neat feeling to know that maybe there's someone out there that thinks the same way you do," she explained. "So I was going to give him the doll and I was going to explain it to him and see what he thought. . . . I hope that I haven't caused him any inconvenience with all this. I never thought this would happen. I never expected to be caught . . . so I hope that he isn't angry with me."[34]

THE PROM MOM
TEEN ADMITS KILLING BABY AT HIGH SCHOOL DANCE

On her way to her high school prom in Forked River, New Jersey, Melissa Drexler started having cramps while riding in her boyfriend's car. She was nine months pregnant, but she had successfully hidden her condition from everyone, including her boyfriend. Once she arrived at the prom, she acted as if nothing was wrong.

When the cramps increased in intensity, Drexler left the dance floor and went to the ladies' room. While there, she delivered a male child, allowing him to drop into the toilet. She removed the child from the toilet, wrapped him in plastic garbage bags, and deposited him in a trash can. Then she returned to the dance floor, acting as if nothing had happened.

When police found the baby, he was dead, and he had marks on his neck consistent with wounds that are found on strangulation victims. To the surprise of everyone in the community, police arrested Drexler and charged her with murder.

On August 20, 1998, Melissa Drexler went before a judge and pleaded guilty to a lesser charge of aggravated manslaughter. Her plea was part of an agreement worked out between her lawyers and prosecutors.

"I knowingly took the baby out of the toilet and wrapped a series of garbage bags around [him]," Drexler told the court. "I was aware of what I was doing at the time when I placed the baby in the bag, and I was further aware that what I did would most certainly result in the death of the baby."

The judge sentenced her to fifteen years in prison.

With tears in her eyes, Drexler apologized for her actions.

THE APOLOGY

"I'd like to tell you I'm really, truly sorry for what I've done. Okay?"[35]

WYATT EARP

WILD WEST LAWMAN DRAGGED THROUGH THE MUD

By the turn of the century, Wyatt Earp was the most famous lawman to emerge from the turbulent 1880s and 1890s. His exploits in the Wild West cow towns of Wichita and Dodge City had made him a legend even before he moved to Tombstone, Arizona.

However, history probably best remembers Earp for his role in the gunfight at OK Corral, at which Earp, his brothers, and their friend Doc Holliday shot it out with the Clanton gang on the streets of Tombstone.

Earp never recovered from the notoriety.

The final years of his life were spent in San Francisco, where he struggled to make a living and fought to keep his head above the reputation he had earned as a lawman and gunfighter.

One day he was asked to be the referee at a boxing match. Prizefighting was illegal in San Francisco at that time, but law-enforcement officials always looked the other way. Earp's decision to referee the prize fight was tantamount, by today's standards, to joining the World Wrestling Federation.

For reasons known only to Earp, he tucked his six-shooter (one witness later described it as being "a foot long") into his vest. When fight officials spotted the gun, he was asked to surrender it, which he did without making a scene.

Unfortunately, the fight ended badly and there were charges that Earp was part of a con-spiracy to fix the fight in the winner's favor. He was never charged with conspiracy—that would have been tough since the fight itself was illegal—but he was charged with carrying a concealed weapon.

At his trial, Earp, at forty-eight years of age, was the very picture of a broken man. He got confused on the witness stand, couldn't remember names, and admitted to the world that he was living in poverty. He was hardly the dashing figure depicted in the legend of the Gunfight at OK Corral.

The trial made front-page headlines across the nation.

Aside from the embarrassment of being charged, the former lawman's worst moment came when he missed a court date and was asked by the judge to apologize in open court. It was a humiliating moment for Earp.

The judge accepted his apology.

When the trial concluded, the judge issued his ruling. Since prizefights were illegal, he said, he would be hard-pressed to either convict or exonerate Earp since his possession of a gun was linked to the fight itself. He dismissed the charges.

Earp walked out of the court a free man, but he never recovered, financially or personally, from the bad publicity. He died in 1929.

THE APOLOGY

"Well, I must apologize humbly for my neglect," Earp told the judge. "You see, when the officer served me, I was very busy with some telegrams at the Baldwin. I thoughtlessly put the subpoena in my pocket, thinking that I would attend to it later, and then clean forgot all about it. I am very sorry."

"It is a very peculiar thing that you should forget the service of a subpoena," said the judge.

"That is so, Your Honor, but really, I was so much engaged in talking about the fight, that the whole matter was driven out of my head. I can assure you that I did not mean any disrespect. Why, I have been an officer for twenty years myself, and know what a serious thing it is to disobey the order of the court. I beg your pardon, Your Honor, I'm sure."[36]

THE CASINO MURDER
CHILD KILLER DAMNED IN HIS OWN MIND

On Memorial Day weekend 1997, Jeremy Strohmeyer and his high school buddy, David Cash, went to a gambling resort in Primma, Nevada, where they joined Cash's father for an evening of gambling and video games.

While in the casino, Strohmeyer saw seven-year-old Sherrice Iverson duck into a rest room while her father played the slot machines upstairs. Strohmeyer followed her into the rest room and raped her, holding his hand over the little girl's mouth to muffle her screams. After the assault, he killed the little girl and rejoined his friend in the casino.

Strohmeyer subsequently was arrested and charged with the little girl's murder. Before the trial began, he pleaded guilty to kidnapping and murder as part of a plea-bargain agreement designed to avoid the death penalty. He was sentenced to life imprisonment without parole.

Strohmeyer made his first apology in the courtroom, where he was allowed to make a statement before the judge who imposed the sentence.

THE APOLOGY

"Nobody can really know the sorrow, the guilt, the pain I carry out, except maybe her parents, my parents. I'm going away to prison for the rest of my life, and that's only fair."

Later, in an interview with Barbara Walters for ABC TV, he apologized again when Walters asked him if he felt any remorse over the murder.

"Yes, very much so. I'm damned in my own mind. I will never be able to escape the fact that I did this, and every day it hurts."[37]

BUTCH CASSIDY

OUTLAW TURNS DOWN SEX FROM PARTNER'S WIFE

At the turn of the century, Butch Cassidy (a.k.a. Robert LeRoy Parker) and the Sundance Kid (a.k.a. Harry Longabaugh) were nationwide celebrities as members of the Wild Bunch gang, thanks, in part, to the zeal of Wild West–obsessed newspapers in the East that made the men's train and bank robberies front-page news.

By the 1920s the exploits of Butch Cassidy and the Sundance Kid had been relegated to the back pages of history books, where they stayed for half a century. Then along came the movie *Butch Cassidy and the Sundance Kid*, starring Paul Newman and Robert Redford. Almost overnight, the two outlaws, long since dead and buried, again became celebrities, though exactly when they died remains a mystery.

Butch Cassidy was born of devout Mormon parents. Throughout his "career" as an outlaw, he seemed to fight against those early religious influences, but occasionally they arose in his dealings with other people, especially women.

He never married, but he maintained a rather serious fondness for female company. Saying no to a woman was not in his nature.

Once, when one of the members of his gang, Matt Warner, was arrested and held in a Utah jail, Butch Cassidy paid for one of the top criminal attorneys in the West to defend him. Cassidy told friends he was not planning a jailbreak and would rescue Warner "only if money could not do it."

At one point, Cassidy received a letter from Warner's wife, Rosa, promising him "anything he wanted" from her or her sister if he would come and see her. Cassidy told members of the gang that he thought it was a trap, since Rosa was a "loose woman" who wanted her husband to go to jail so that she could carry on with other men.

Cassidy turned down her offer of sex with her and her sister, but it is the manner in which he apologized for not accepting the offer that shows insight into those early childhood Mormon influences.

THE APOLOGY

"My Dear Friend," Butch Cassidy wrote in his letter to Rosa Warner. "Through the kindness of Mrs. Rummel [Cassidy had friends scattered across the territory who received letters for him] I received your letter last night. I am sorry that I can't comply with your request, but at present it is impossible for me to go to see you, and I can't tell just when I can get there."

Cassidy then informed her, using the most polite language imaginable, that he had heard that she really was not interested in seeing her husband set free.

"But that is neither here nor there, you are a lady, and I would do all I could for you or any of the sex that was in trouble, of course. I am foolish (which you have found out), but it is my nature and I can't change it. I may be wrong in this, but if so, I hope you will look over it and prove to me that you are all right, and I will ask forgiveness for writing you as I have. I understand you and Matt named your boy Rex Leroy after me, thank you. . . . Believe me to be a true friend to my kind of people."[38]

AUTUMN JACKSON
"OH, MY PAPA" STRIKES SOUR NOTE

Entertainer Bill Cosby admitted to having an affair with Autumn Jackson's mother nearly twenty-five years ago in a Las Vegas hotel room, but he denied ever being her child's father. But since it was no secret that Cosby paid the mother more than one hundred thousand dollars in financial support, Jackson was convinced he was her father.

Over the years, Cosby tried to convince her otherwise.

"I will be for you a father figure," he told her, "but I am not your father."

Their relationship took an ugly turn in early 1997, when Jackson, then twenty-two, hatched a scheme with the help of a fifty-year-old friend, Jose Medina, to extort money from the entertainer. If he did not pay her forty million dollars, she told him, she would give the story to the tabloids.

Cosby went to the police.

The following year, Autumn Jackson and Jose Medina were both convicted of extortion, conspiracy, and crossing state lines to commit a crime. Jackson was sentenced to twenty-six months in prison.

Before hearing her sentence, Jackson stood before the court and apologized.

> ### THE APOLOGY
>
> "I've had a long time to think about what I've done, and I'd like to apologize to the court and Mr. Cosby. I only hoped that Mr. Cosby would be here and I would be able to apologize to him in person for letting him down . . . and causing his family so much pain."
>
> She told the court she had recently married and wanted to start a family.
>
> "I knew Mr. Cosby held great expectations for me and believed in me when no one else would, and I let him down," she continued. "I'm so sorry."[39]

Chapter 4

Sex, Drugs, and Rock 'n' Roll

MICHAEL JACKSON
EX–POP STAR LEARNS HISTORY LESSON

For nearly a decade after his album *Thriller*, which sold over twenty-five million copies, Michael Jackson was on top of the world. He was the undisputed King of Pop.

Then came news in 1993 that the Santa Barbara sheriff's department was investigating allegations that Jackson had sexually molested a thirteen-year-old boy. The eighth-grader, who frequently traveled with the singer, reported acts of fondling and oral sex to the Santa Barbara Department of Children's Services.

A civil lawsuit was filed by the child's parents.

To deny the allegations, Jackson addressed the nation on live television.

"I am not guilty of these allegations, but if I am guilty of anything, it is of giving all that I have to give to help children all over the world."

One month later, Jackson settled the lawsuit for a reported twenty million dollars, and the investigation was dropped by the Santa Barbara Sheriff's Department when the victim became a reluctant witness.

Michael focused all his attention on making a new album.

When the album, titled *HIStory*, was released in 1995, Jackson thought he had put all his troubles behind him. Not until the first single was played on the radio did it become apparent that Jackson's real troubles were just beginning.

The song, "They Don't Care About Us," came under immediate attack from Jewish groups because of lyrics that referred to Jews as "kikes" and otherwise depicted Jews in a derogatory way. Even the song title was suspect: "They Don't Care About Us" has long been part of the African American lexicon, as applied to Jews. Suddenly, Jackson had to fight for his professional life.

Jackson also went on *PrimeTime Live*, where he was interviewed by television commentator Diane Sawyer. He mentioned his friendship with movie mogul Steven Spielberg, who had written flattering liner notes for the album, as proof of his friendship with Jews. "I could never be a racist," he told Sawyer. "I love all races of people, from Arabs to Jews."

Wait a minute, Spielberg later said to reporters. His comments in the liner notes, he explained, were written in 1993, before he ever heard the music in the album.

Despite one of the most expensive marketing campaigns in history—more than thirty-five million dollars was spent on advertising—*HIStory* sold an embarrassing two million copies. The album did not even earn enough to pay expenses.

THE APOLOGY

"There has been a lot of controversy about my song, 'They Don't Care About Us.' My intention was for this song to say 'no' to racism, anti-Semitism, and stereotyping. Unfortunately, my choice of words may have unintentionally hurt the very people I wanted to stand in solidarity with. I just want you all to know how strongly I am committed to tolerance, peace and love, and apologize to anyone who might have been hurt."[40]

COURTNEY LOVE
MAGAZINE BITCH-SLAPS EX-QUEEN OF GRUNGE

Courtney Love is one of those women people love to hate.

Whether it is because they feel she was involved somehow in the untimely demise of her husband, beloved grunge rocker Kurt Cobain, or because she *really* let herself go during her lipstick-smeared years, or—worse yet—because she sought respectability as a legitimate actress in *The People vs. Larry Flynt*, Love has been blessed with a larger-than-average negative public opinion rating.

When she was asked to do a major interview for *Spin* magazine, she viewed it as an opportunity to not only plug her band's new album, *Celebrity Skin*, but to mend some fences and perhaps issue an apology or two.

Love told the interviewer that when she looks at old pictures of herself in ripped clothes and smeared mascara, she feels ashamed. So she's sorry about all that unpleasantness, okay?

Then, having set the record straight on that phase of her life, she apologized for allowing her handlers to seduce her into posing for a series of glamorous Versace clothing ads. She's sorry about going through that whole glam phase. Her fans can rest assured *that* will never happen again, okay?

Finally, she apologized to her fans for not having the courage to allow her armpit hair to grow out. There are some things she won't do for art's sake, okay?

Imagine her surprise, then, when the October 1998 issue of *Spin* hit the newsstands with cover lines that branded her as a "Sellout, Bitch, Killer." In a letter to the editor in chief of *Spin,* Michael Hirschorn, the mortified Love demanded an apology.

Michael Hirschorn really had nowhere to go.

The article itself was not controversial. Love was cooperative with the interviewer and did her best to play the role of a mainstream rocker. At times she even projected images of sweetness. One would like to have been a fly on the wall when she saw the cover of the magazine.

In the November 1998 issue of the magazine, Hirschorn printed a red-ink apology.

THE APOLOGY

"Our October cover story on the return of Hole was not controversial, but the cover line drew an impassioned response from people who took issue with the highly charged language of the cover lines.

"The feeling was that by airing the worst accusations that have been made against Courtney Love, even if only to debunk them, *Spin's* cover validated those charges. . . . Our cover line may have been journalistically sound, but it lacked in humanity . . . throwing the language on the cover, out of context, was just plain hurtful. I have apologized to [her] personally and would like to use this public forum to apologize to her publicly."

MARILYN MONROE
"NO ONE WILL EVER KNOW"

It must have seemed like a good idea at the time.

In May 1949, Marilyn Monroe showed up unannounced at the studio of Hollywood photographer Tom Kelley and explained that she was looking for work as a model. Kelley told her that her timing was absolutely perfect. The model he had hired for a Pabst beer poster had not shown up and he needed a stand-in.

Kelley shot a photo of Monroe in a one-piece swimsuit with a beach ball.

At the end of the session, Kelley paid Monroe for her services and told her he would give her a call if anything else came up. Pabst lost no time getting the poster in production, and within a couple of weeks it was being distributed nationwide.

Spotting the poster was a Chicago calendar manufacturer, who called Kelley and asked if Monroe would pose nude for an artfully rendered calendar. At first, Monroe told Kelley she did not think it would be good for her career. "It pays fifty dollars," he countered. "Besides, no one will ever know. Your name won't be on it."

Monroe desperately needed the money, so she said yes.

Kelley posed her on a red velvet drape he spread out on the studio floor. Monroe stretched out on her left side, arms extended past her head, in a pose that showed off her perfectly toned twenty-two-year-old figure. When Kelley saw the photographs, he was stunned. Monroe was pretty enough in person, but on film she was . . . well, magical!

Monroe used the money to pay her bills and forgot about the photographs. Three years later, she was well on her way as an actress after being signed to a movie contract with Fox. As was the custom in those days, Fox loaned her out to another studio, RKO, for a movie titled *Clash by Night.*

Before the movie was released, someone told RKO executives about the nude photographs. The movie studio saw an opportunity to use the photographs as a publicity stunt to attract attention to *Clash by Night.*

Posing nude for a calendar was not something actresses did in the 1950s if they wanted to have a career in the movies. Since RKO's loyalty was to the movie—and not to Monroe's long-term career—it provided reporters with copies of the calendar and full details of the photo session. The scandal made front-page news across the country.

To counter the wave of negative publicity, Monroe held a press conference.

Monroe's honest admission of guilt caught America off guard. It allowed every woman who had ever transgressed the nation's rigid 1950s sexual boundaries and every man who had ever had a lustful thought (or action) to feel good about themselves.

Fox executives received an avalanche of mail in support of the repentant actress. Of that very public apology, a star of the first magnitude was born—and America, to its surprise, found itself in love with a fallen woman![41]

THE APOLOGY

Yes, she admitted to reporters, she did indeed pose nude for the calendar. "I was a week behind in my rent at the Studio Club," she said. "I had to have fifty dollars, and the photographer, Tom Kelley, didn't think that anyone would recognize me."

Besides, she added with breathless conviction, "I was hungry!"

GEORGE JONES
A BIRD IN THE HAND IS WORTH . . .

For most of his career, country star George Jones was a heavy drinker.

He'd be the first to tell you that was true. Thankfully, for both himself and his fans, he was able to pull his life together and get on with the business of making music. He hasn't gone on a serious drinking jag in years. At least that's his story—and he's sticking to it, despite pleading guilty in 1999 to driving while impaired.

One of the worst things about sobering up, he writes in his autobiography, *I Lived to Tell It All*, is remembering all the goofy, unpardonable, mean-spirited things that were done under the influence of alcohol. At the top of that list is what he did to Grand Ole Opry star Porter Wagoner.

Jones and his wife, Tammy Wynette, were performing at the Opry, which in those days was located in Ryman Auditorium. During a break, Jones saw Wagoner head for the men's room. He had already consumed his share of alcohol and diet pills on that day.

For some reason, Jones had it in his head that Wagoner and Wynette were seeing each other romantically behind his back. That was why he followed Wagoner into the men's room. He wanted to confront him over this imaginary affair.

Jones walked up behind Wagoner, who was standing at the urinal, and he reached around and grabbed his penis. "I want to see what Tammy's so proud of!" he said.

"I twisted hard," Jones recalled in his autobiography. "Porter began to jump and wave his arms. His sequin suit made him a blur of shimmering silver. He doesn't move much onstage. He moves a lot when you pinch his penis."

Wagoner urinated on himself and had to change clothes before the next show.

Later, Jones learned he had accused an innocent man.

Most sensible people would consider grabbing a man's penis—and then twisting it real hard—an offense deserving of an apology, even if the man is guilty of Heaven knows what. But grabbing the penis of an innocent man! That's not something that is easily forgotten or forgiven.

Twenty-five years later, when Jones's co-writer, Tom Carter, asked Wagoner about the incident for the book, the performer recounted the incident in rich detail. At the end of their conversation, he said he would call Carter in a couple of days and give him some more stories. He never did.

> ### THE APOLOGY
>
> "The next time I saw Porter I was sober, apologetic, and very humble," Jones wrote in his autobiography. "'Hey, man,'" Jones recalled him saying, "'that behavior wasn't you. That was a drunk man. I forgive you.'"

"He said he forgave me, and maybe he did," said Jones. "But he didn't forget. . . . Imagine having a friend for four decades whose only pointed recollection for publication is that you twisted his [penis]."[42]

VANESSA WILLIAMS
MISS AMERICA GOES DOWN WITH AMAZING GRACE

Representing the state of New York, Vanessa Williams made history when she was chosen Miss America of 1984. She was the first African American woman to ever wear the coveted beauty pageant crown.

Less than a year later, her world crumbled when she learned that *Penthouse* magazine planned to publish nude photos of her that were taken fourteen months before she became Miss America.

At the time the photographs were taken, she worked as a receptionist for a freelance photographer named Dennis Dowdell. One day he wanted to do a nude, girl-on-girl layout, but he had only one model, a languid, long-legged blonde. He asked Williams, who was twenty at the time, if she would mind posing with the other woman. Since Williams had ambitions of becoming a model, she said yes.

Both models were nude throughout the session. The photographs were meant to depict a lesbian relationship between a black woman and a white woman, but they were tame by industry standards. The touching was implied and not actual.

Once Dowdell learned Williams had been crowned Miss America, he contacted *Penthouse*. The magazine was delighted to publish the photographs, the first ever of a Miss America in the buff.

At a July 1984 press conference, Williams surrendered her crown at the pageant's request, making history, yet again, as she became the first reigning Miss America to ever step down in disgrace for showing off the body that won her the crown.

Although privately she felt it was she who was due an apology—she said she never meant for the photographs to be published—Vanessa Williams stood before reporters with dignity and grace, and she offered a public apology for embarrassing the pageant with the photographs.

Williams was replaced as Miss America by Miss New Jersey, a perky, twenty-one-year-old who had been chosen first runner-up during the contest, but it was Williams who went on to fame and fortune in the 1990s as an award-winning singer and actress.[43]

THE APOLOGY

"It is apparent to me now that because of all that has happened during the past week, it would be difficult to make appearances as Miss America. The potential harm to the pageant and the deep division that a bitter fight may cause has convinced me that I must relinquish my title as Miss America."

Williams told of the anguish she felt over the incident: "It is one thing to face up to a mistake that one makes in youth, but it has been almost totally devastating to have to share it with the American public and the world at large."

JERRY LEE LEWIS
KILLER TRIES TO EAT HIS OWN WORDS

Jerry Lee Lewis stood outside Sun Records studio during a break in a 1985 recording session. It was the first time in many years that the "Killer" had been inside the legendary studio. With him was a reporter who had been invited to the session. After a few minutes of conversation, the reporter pulled out a miniature tape recorder and began to interview the rock 'n' roller who had once dominated the record charts with hits such as "Great Balls of Fire."

For the first few questions, everything seemed fine.

The reporter had used the same tape recorder to interview Lewis on previous occasions. It was a routine interview in many respects: just a few questions about what it felt like to return to the studio that had made him an international star.

Suddenly, without warning, Lewis snapped.

The singer's eyes glazed over. Without warning, he grabbed the tape recorder and tried to wrench it from the reporter's hand. That proved difficult, since the tape recorder had a strap that the reporter had looped over his finger. As horrified onlookers stood frozen in place, the singer and the reporter grappled over the tape recorder, their feet slashing about in the gravel of the parking lot.

Lewis's manager, an earnest man by the name of J. W., ran from the other side of the parking lot, screaming out his client's name. At about that time, the strap and the bottom part of the tape recorder broke. Lewis stepped away, his eyes fierce and unforgiving. He held the tape recorder in his hand, gazing at it as if he could not believe he really had it, then, without a word, he raised it to his mouth and began chewing on it, his teeth nipping away at the metallic casing as if it were an ear of buttered corn.

J. W. took the tape recorder away from Lewis and gave it to the reporter, then he escorted Lewis to the other side of the parking lot, where he engaged him in a few minutes of animated conversation. Then J. W. struck out across the parking lot, toting an apology that seemed to grow heavier with each step he took.

"Jerry wants to apologize. He'd like to buy you a new tape recorder."

"No, thanks," said the reporter. "It's not broken."

J. W. relayed the message to Lewis. A few minutes later, he returned with an even grander apology. "Jerry really feels bad," he explained. "He'd like to buy you a couple of new recorders. That way, you'll have a spare."

The reporter shook his head.

J. W., beginning to appear a little frayed about the edges, took the bad news back to Lewis. The reporter watched as the conversation between the two men grew even more animated. J. W. threw up his hands and stomped across the parking lot with yet another offer. "Jerry wants to buy you a hundred new

THE APOLOGY

Face-to-face with the reporter, Lewis reached out to shake his hand.

"I'm sorry, man," he said, his eyes lowered in embarrassment.[44]

recorders," he said, his eyes pleading for acceptance. Again, the reporter said no.

Frustrated, J. W. retraced his steps, this time walking so slowly he seemed to be dragging his feet. He told Lewis what the reporter said. This time, it was Lewis who threw up his arms. He paced back and forth, walking in circles around J. W. Then, abruptly, he turned and headed back across the parking lot toward the reporter, his arms swinging at his side.

FIONA APPLE
SINGER TWISTED INTO KNOTS BY PANTY ANGST

When the waiflike teen exploded on the pop scene in 1996 with her debut album, *Tidal*, no one knew quite what to think about Fiona Apple. Her music was solid—jazz-influenced pop tunes that displayed musical sophistication and lyrical depth—but there was something about the singer that made everyone uncomfortable.

Then the story about her record deal came out. She was no struggling artist who had paid her dues in smoky nightclubs. Her success seemed to be a fluke. She made a demo tape and gave it to a girlfriend, who gave it to a music publicist she baby-sat for.

Suddenly, Apple had a record deal, without really trying.

When she started doing interviews to promote the album, the music somehow got lost as music writers focused on her fragile, marble-eyed beauty and her tale of being raped at the tender age of twelve.

With the release of the video for the song "Criminal," the media became obsessed with her kiddie-porn look, and all reporters could think and write about was this haunting, nineteen-year-old beauty who was strutting about in her underwear, wearing her adolescent angst not on her sleeve but on the crotch of her panties.

Apple's shining moment came in 1997 when she received MTV's Best New Artist Award. She knew it was because of the video, so when she took the stage to accept the award she told the audience that people were fools to pattern their lives on what pop stars told them was cool. She was politely ignored by the audience.

Once sales for *Tidal* went down, Apple disappeared from public view. Fans didn't know whether she was holed up somewhere trying to slit her wrists or whether she was recording a new album. As it turned out, she was not slitting her wrists.

To everyone's surprise, Apple emerged in late 1999 with a new album. Titled *When the Pawn . . .* , it received excellent reviews, most of which focused on the musical content of the album. To her relief, no one seemed concerned about her panty angst.

Once she hit the interview trail again, the first thing she did was to apologize for wearing her panties in the video. She was convinced she had won the MTV award solely because of her panties. She *needed* to apologize to someone.

THE APOLOGY

"But what f***ing bullshit did I win that award for? I won because of the video for 'Criminal,' and because it was controversial. I won for being in my underwear on MTV. And that made me so ashamed of myself."

Apple said she regretted ever making that video.

"Me making that video was me going, 'I want to be the person that people want to see in her underwear.' I rationalized doing it because I didn't want to say no to anybody, and because it fed my ego."[45]

PRINCESS STEPHANIE
BODYGUARD-HUSBAND CAN'T EXPLAIN NUDITY

Monaco's Prince Rainier probably wasn't too happy when his youngest daughter, Princess Stephanie, told him she wanted to marry Daniel Ducruet, a former bodyguard, but the marriage was allowed to take place.

Daniel Ducruet is no Grace Kelly, that's for sure.

That's why it probably came as no surprise to Prince Rainier when nude photographs of Ducruet and a twenty-six-year-old stripper appeared in tabloids all over the world. The couple had been caught by a hidden photographer as they cavorted poolside at a Riviera villa. Ducruet said it was all a big mistake.

Not persuaded was Princess Stephanie, who filed for divorce.

Ducruet quickly learned he was the most hated man in Monaco.

In an effort to set things right with his wife—and, just as important to him, the public—he confessed his feelings of guilt and shame to the tabloid *Hello!*

THE APOLOGY

"I've betrayed my wife, I've betrayed her love, and, above all, I've betrayed my children, who are going to have to bear the consequences."

Ducruet said he met the stripper while he was on holiday. He said she told him she was depressed because of problems with her boyfriend and needed comforting. "I got there, she threw herself at me, crying, and I comforted her. We had a drink and then another one. I lost my self-control."

Asked about his nudity, Ducruet said he really couldn't explain that.[46]

SEAN "PUFFY" COMBS
RAPMEISTER MORPHS INTO ROUGH DADDY

Not long after Sean "Puffy" Combs made a cameo appearance in a 1999 video for a song recorded by fellow rapper Nas, he had second thoughts and asked Interscope Records executive Steve Stoute to delete the scene before it aired.

To Combs's surprise, the video aired with the offending scene intact.

Thirty minutes after seeing the video on MTV, Combs and several of his bodyguards entered the record label's Manhattan offices, according to Stoute's statement to police, and proceeded to punch him in the face and beat him to the ground with a telephone. The attack continued, said Stoute, with Combs's accomplices joining in, kicking him and pummeling him with a chair and their fists.

Subsequently, Combs was arrested and charged with second-degree assault and criminal mischief. On the eve of his court hearing, Combs made a public apology to Stoute.

THE APOLOGY

"I'm extremely sorry for what I did. I messed up. It's nobody's fault but my own. I'm not apologizing so that I won't go to jail or so I won't get sued. I've told Steve I'm truly sorry, and I mean it."

Combs said he was embarrassed about the incident.

"I made a mistake. I disappointed myself. I disappointed my family. I disappointed Bertelsmann and Seagram [record company owners] and many people who believed in me. I'm looked up to. I'm supposed to be a leader in the world of hip-hop. And I disappointed everybody. Hip-hop was practically violence-free for a couple years there, and I put a scuff on it. For me to do something this stupid was really dumb. I can't say I'm sorry enough."[47]

TOMMY LEE

MAYBE NOT THE ONE YOU REALLY WANT TO HEAR

Mötley Crüe drummer Tommy Lee seems to have problems with his temper.

That's not unusual with drummers. It is said that the two professions that best reflect repressed anger are butcher and rock 'n' roll drummer.

If the changes in Lee's music career don't work out—he left Mötley Crüe to pursue what has become a full-time career as on-again-off-again husband to media mogul Pamela Anderson Lee—then someone, *please,* get the man a meat cleaver and show him how to use it in a socially accepted manner.

There are at least three apologies Lee desperately needs to make, but so far he has issued only one— to a freelance photographer he attacked outside a nightclub. The photographer re-ceived a broken pelvis and a broken rib from the attack.

Lee's apology to the freelance photographer occurred on the steps of the courthouse. The musician was leaving the building when he was stopped by reporters, who asked if he had anything to say about the incident.

Apologies eagerly awaited, but not yet offered, include: one for his part in inciting a racially motivated riot during a 1997 concert in North Carolina (for which he was subsequently charged with felony and misdemeanor offenses); and the other for allegedly attacking Pamela while she was holding their then-seven-week-old child.

For the second, he did give sort of an explanation to reporters for the television tabloid *Extra*: "I didn't know what to do while I was being hit in the face. . . ."[48]

THE APOLOGY

"I'd like to say I'm sorry to Mr. Trappler [the photographer], actually. I've never formally gotten a chance to say I'm sorry."

THE DUCHESS OF YORK
FERGIE GIVES TOE SUCKING A BAD NAME

British tabloids are different from their American counterparts in two major respects: They run photos of bare-breasted women on a regular basis, and they saturate their pages with articles about the Royal Family.

No one understands that better than Sarah Ferguson, perhaps better known as "Fergie," the Duchess of York and the former wife of Prince Andrew. So what was she thinking in the summer of 1992 when she went on holiday in the south of France with an American named John Bryan?

Fergie wasn't just any married woman. She was the wife of the Duke of York—the mother of two daughters, princesses who are fifth and sixth in line to the throne. Naturally, the British tabloids put photographers on her trail when they got wind of the tryst. It was the story of the decade.

Hoping to get lucky, the tabloids stationed photographers around the hideaway where Fergie and her American friend vacationed. The payoff exceeded their wildest dreams. Photographers snapped photographs of Fergie sitting topless next to the American, and they got shots of them cuddling on a lounge chair.

Photographs of a topless princess were bad enough, but that wasn't the worst of it. One of the photographs showed the American apparently sucking Fergie's toes. For a time, it was a toss-up over which was worse for the image of the Royal Family: photographs of the princess's breasts or photographs of her allowing her toes to be sucked by an American.

The British tabs ran both photographs, but it was the toe-sucking episode that seemed to attract the most attention.

FERGIE'S STOLEN KISSES read the headlines.

It's hard to imagine anything worse could have happened to Fergie.

She and Prince Andrew had been talking about a separation, but nothing definite had been decided. Then came the tabloid headlines and the shame of having her breasts viewed by the royal subjects—and then there was the toe sucking, which she maintains to this day was nothing more than innocent toe kissing.

THE APOLOGY

"I still had to face the woman by whose kind permission I was staying at Balmoral. She was my mother-in-law and my Sovereign, and a woman I cared about deeply."

Fergie told the Queen she was sorry.

"The Queen was furious. I had apologized, of course, but penance and contrition have their limits—there are some things which cannot be put right."

For the remainder of the day, Fergie apologized to every other family member she encountered, even Prince Philip, who, to her surprise, tried to console her. That evening, when she entered the room for dinner, she felt everyone, even the servants, were staring at her breasts. "I felt naked in their sight. I would need a *Roget's* to express my degradation at that moment, and even then I would fail . . . there are no words for it."[49]

GARTH BROOKS
ROAD ROMANCES HOBBLE COUNTRY CROONER

You wouldn't know it to look at him, but Garth Brooks—all two-hundred-plus pounds of him—once had a thing for the ladies. All those feminine overtures at the concerts, the panties and bras tossed up on the stage, the requests for autographs on body parts, all were more than he could resist. So he didn't!

When his wife Sandy learned of his infidelities on the road, she called him and confronted him with it. It was November 1989 and he was getting ready to go onstage.

"I told him my bags were packed, my plane ticket's bought, and I'm gone," she later told reporters. Garth begged for a chance to explain. He denied having affairs on the road. Sandy told him he would have to come home, where they could talk "eye to eye."

That night at the concert, Garth sang his hit "If Tomorrow Never Comes," choking up when he came to the parts he felt applied to his relationship with Sandy. He stopped singing, weeping right there on stage.

"Man, sometimes the road is just pure hell on a marriage," he told the audience, then started the song over. That night, after the concert, he boarded a small plane that had been hired to take him to his next gig.

As soon as the plane landed, Garth ran to a telephone and called Sandy. He told her he had lied when he denied having the affairs. He wanted to make it right with her. The long distance confession and apology must have worked, for Sandy was waiting for him when he got home.

THE APOLOGY

"I wore out a pair of jeans in the knees crawling behind her, trying to get her to stay. Oh, man, I never cried so much in my whole life, never begged so much. The day she told me she would come back is the day I started to become the husband I needed to be."[50]

JOHN MICHAEL MONTGOMERY
DEAR MOM: YOUR SERVICES ARE NO LONGER NEEDED

Country singer John Michael Montgomery, whose hits include "Angel in My Eyes," has done well for himself with songs that extol the "old" American virtues of love of family and country.

The thirty-three-year-old singer was so old-fashioned that he put his mother in charge of his fan club. Imagine the fans' surprise when they received a letter in 1999 from Montgomery's mother saying that she had been fired.

That didn't seem to bother her so much as did the way in which she was notified—by mail. In her final newsletter, she said: "I have held off publishing the newsletter hoping he would change his mind or give me some kind of explanation . . . [but] he hasn't even talked to me about it."

Montgomery was besieged with questions about the way he treated his mom.

Unfortunately, Montgomery's spat with his mom was the least of his worries.

The singer's stepmother sued him in a Kentucky court because he used his dead father's image and voice in a video. It was his stepmother's position that she controlled the estate of Montgomery's father and no one had asked for her permission to place her late husband in a video.

The court ruled in the stepmother's favor, but an appeals court later overturned that verdict, saying, in effect, that the father was never famous enough to have commercial value.

THE APOLOGY

"I regret this has become such a fiasco. But I give my word to my fans, I will sit down with my mom and we will work this out between us."[51]

PAUL McCARTNEY
EX-BEATLE TAKES HIT FOR FUSSY NATURE

In the beginning they called Paul McCartney the "pretty" Beatle, but a more apt description might have been the "sensitive" Beatle, or the "mother" Beatle, for it was Paul, more so than the others, who fretted and stayed up at night, worrying about the future of their musical family.

When McCartney filed a lawsuit asking for the dissolution of the Beatles partnership, the media and some of the Beatles themselves interpreted his action as an attack against the Beatle "family."

Nothing could have been further from the truth.

Ringo, George, and John had already left the group, and although Ringo and George eventually returned, John did not. That uncertainty had left their legal partnership in never-never land, where wolves were already circling the camp.

Paul's plan was to destroy the Beatles in an effort to save them.

Many angry words were exchanged by the Beatles through their lawyers, most of which were directed at Paul. He overlooked most of what was said, but when he read Ringo's legal deposition, something his old mate said struck a chord with him.

"Paul is the greatest bass guitar player in the world," said Ringo in the deposition. "He is also very determined. He goes on and on to see if he can get his own way. While this may be a virtue, it did mean that musical disagreements inevitably rose from time to time. But such disagreements contributed to really great products. . . . My own view is that all four of us together could even yet work out everything satisfactory."

McCartney was stunned by Ringo's comments.

Perhaps to prove Ringo wrong, he went back and listened to outtakes from some of their early songs, tapes that had been kept running and allowed their conversations to be recorded. What he heard surprised him.

The phrases "he is also very determined" and "he goes on and on to see if he can get his own way" possessed so much truth that McCartney felt compelled to apologize.

THE APOLOGY

"Looking back on it now, I can say, 'Yes, okay, in the studio I could be overbearing.' Because I wanted to get it right! I heard tapes recently of me counting in 'I Wanna Hold Your Hand,' which was our first number one in the States, and I'm being pretty bossy: 'Sssh, Sssh! Clean beginning, c'mon everyone. One, two, no, c'mon, get it right!' and I can see how that could get on your nerves."[52]

GEORGE MICHAEL
SOLO PERFORMANCE LANDS SINGER IN JAIL

A Beverly Hills police officer was patrolling a local park when he stepped into the bathroom and caught a man engaged in what the officer later described as a "lewd act." The man, who identified himself as Georgios Panayiotou, was arrested and booked on suspicion of misdemeanor lewd conduct.

Later, at the jail, Panayiotou admitted to cops that he was George Michael, the pop singer. Panayiotou, he explained, is his actual surname. He was released the same day after posting five hundred dollars bail.

Once the arrest was made public, police were asked by the media exactly what George Michael was doing in the bathroom. They refused to elaborate, saying only that the Grammy-winning singer, whose 1987 hit "I Want Your Sex" was banned by many radio stations, was alone at the time and was witnessed doing *something* by the officer. Michael was subsequently convicted.

In an interview with CNN, Michael apologized to his fans, saying that he embarrassed not only himself but them as well.

THE APOLOGY

"I just want to let them know that I'm okay. I wanted to let them know that this is not going to finish me off."

Michael said it wasn't the first time something like that had happened.

"I put myself in an extremely stupid and vulnerable position, especially because I'm in the privileged position that I am.

I've put myself in that position before."

Michael described his sexuality as "ambiguous."

"I want to say that I have no problem with people knowing that I'm in a relationship with a man right now. I have not been in a relationship with a woman for almost ten years."[53]

MARILYN MANSON
GOTH REVERSAL OF MOMMIE DEAREST

For the latter part of the 1990s, rocker Marilyn Manson was one of the most controversial musicians on the concert circuit. Whether it was because of the violence critics attributed to his music or because of his heavily made-up Goth appearance or because of the bizarre imagery he espoused—the cover on his album *Mechanical Animals* depicted the pasty singer naked, with prosthetic breasts—he was a lightning rod for those who felt American music had descended straight into hell.

Was Manson's imagery based on fact or fiction? In his autobiography, Manson admitted that in his youth he physically attacked his mother by hitting her, spitting on her, and choking her during violent outbursts. Critics were not surprised by those disclosures, since they seemed to be in character with their image of Manson, but the singer's apology for those actions probably was unexpected.

THE APOLOGY

"At one particularly rebellious period of my life, I was very violent with my mother. I think it was something I got from my father, both emotionally and physically, because they were having problems and I thought they were going to get a divorce."

Manson said he thought, at the time, that his mother was having an affair. He handled those fears by reacting with violence toward her.

"It's probably one of the only things I regret in life. I have very few moments of remorse, but that's one thing I wish I could take back."[54]

Chapter 5

Politics As the Spice of Life

PRESIDENT BILL CLINTON
MONICA, MONICA, MONICA

It starts out small, as such things are apt to do. The president is named as a defendant in a sexual harassment lawsuit. He begins an affair with a White House intern named Monica L. Lewinsky. He engages in sexual activity in the Oval Office. He lies about having the affair. He gets caught in his lies.

He is impeached by the House of Representatives on charges of perjury and obstruction of justice. The impeachment is turned over to the Senate, which is charged, by the United States Constitution, with conducting a trial, with removal of the president from office as the outcome if he is convicted by the senators.

Clinton is the first elected president to ever undergo such a trial (President Andrew Johnson underwent a trial, but he had ascended to the office and was not elected). Before the trial began, Clinton delivered an apology to the American people, speaking to the White House press corps and a live television audience from a podium in the White House Rose Garden. In the background flapped Old Glory.

History records that Clinton ultimately escaped being removed from office, but just barely—and some observers credit his apology.

THE APOLOGY

"As anyone close to me knows, for months I have been grappling with how best to reconcile myself to the American people, to acknowledge my own wrongdoing, and still to maintain my focus on the work of the presidency.

"Others are presenting my defense on the facts, the law, and the Constitution. Nothing I can say now can add to that. What I want the American people to know, what I want the Congress to know is that I am profoundly sorry for all I have done wrong in words and deeds. I never should have misled the country, the Congress, my friends, or my family. Quite simply, I gave in to my shame.

"I have been condemned by my accusers with harsh words. And while it's hard to hear yourself called deceitful and manipulative, I remember Ben Franklin's admonition that our critics are our friends, for they do show us our faults.

"Mere words cannot fully express the profound remorse I feel for what our country is going through, and for what members of both parties in Congress are now forced to deal with.

"These past months have been a torturous process of coming to terms with what I did. I understand that accountability demands consequences, and I'm prepared to accept them. Painful though the condemnation of the Congress would be, it would pale in comparison to

the consequences of the pain I have caused my family. There is no greater agony.

"Like anyone who honestly faces the shame of wrongful conduct, I would give anything to go back and undo what I did. But one of the painful truths I have to live with is the reality that that is simply not possible. An old and dear friend of mine recently sent me the wisdom of a poet, who wrote, 'The moving finger writes, and having writ moves on. Nor all your piety, nor wit shall lure it back to cancel half a line. Nor all your tears wash out a word of it.'

"So nothing—not piety, nor tears, nor wit, nor torment—can alter what I have done. I must make my peace with that. I must also be at peace with the fact that the public consequences of my actions are in the hands of the American people and their representatives in the Congress. Should they determine that my errors of word and deed require their rebuke and censure, I am ready to accept that.

"Meanwhile, I will continue to do all I can to reclaim the trust of the American people and to serve them well. We must all return to the work, the vital work, of strengthening our nation for the new century. Our country has wonderful opportunities and daunting challenges ahead. I intend to seize those opportunities and meet those challenges with all the energy and ability and strength God has given me.

"That is simply all I can do—the work of the American people. Thank you very much."

THE BOOZE CRUISE
GOVERNMENT OF THE BREASTS, BY THE DRINK

When Massachusetts governor William Weld appointed Peter Blute to the $120,000-a-year position of state Port Authority director in 1997, the public probably thought Blute would spend most of his time overseeing Logan International Airport and the Port of Boston.

Imagine everyone's surprise, two years later, when Blute authorized the Port Authority to pay for a four-hour cruise for Maureen Stemberg, ex-wife of Thomas Stemberg, the founder of Staples office-supply chain. The purpose of the cruise, he said, was to plan a fund-raiser for a cancer charity.

THE APOLOGY

In his letter of resignation to the governor, Blute said, "Recent errors in judgment by myself have called into question my ability to remain as executive director of this authority."[55]

Whatever the noble purpose of the cruise, it all seemed to fall apart in quick order. Blute and Republican lobbyist Sandy Tennant, who once headed the state Republican Party, were photographed drinking beer and champagne. Toward the end of the cruise, a female passenger lifted her shirt, exposing her breasts, which elicited applause from others on the cruise ship.

Photographs of what became known as the "booze cruise" were published in the *Boston Herald*, prompting Blute to reimburse the Port Authority for the expense of the cruise. He later resigned from his position with the Port Authority.

MAYOR MARION BARRY
CRACK COCAINE SERVED UP IN FBI STING

It's difficult to hold elected office without making enemies, but Mayor Marion Barry—a Memphis-born African American who grew up in a city known for decades as the "murder capital" of America—managed to lead Washington, D.C.'s city government with a minimum amount of constituent disapproval.

In the eyes of some, Barry was a hero. He was praised as a progressive, someone who would lead the city to new and better things.

One day that bubble burst.

In 1990, Barry accompanied a former model to a downtown hotel room, where he smoked crack cocaine. Unknown to Barry, the room was under videotape surveillance by the FBI and his female escort was working with authorities in a sting operation.

Barry was busted and videotape of the incident was given to the news media.

Several months before his court date, Barry went on an apology offensive.

On the *Sally Jesse Raphael Show*, he declared that he suffered from two addictions: drugs and sex. "It was all part of the addiction," he said. "This disease is cunning, baffling, powerful. It destroys your judgment."

Following that appearance, he made back-to-back appearances on local television. In each interview, he offered his "deepest and sincere apologies" to District residents for having embarrassed the city.

In August 1990, Barry was convicted of misdemeanor cocaine possession and sentenced to a six-month prison term. While serving his sentence, he again made headlines when prison officials announced they were investigating reports that Barry had been seen having sex in the visiting room with a female visitor.[56]

THE APOLOGY

"I've caused some pain among people in this city—people who were not necessarily supporters—but who felt for the city. And to those people I offer my deepest and sincere apologies, my sincere regrets, and my feeling of remorse about it.

"I'm not interested in votes at this point. I'm not interested in trying to change voters' minds about Marion Barry's performance or lack thereof. I'm only trying to share with this city my pain, my experience, and my new feelings about the balance of my life."

ROBERT KENNEDY
DROPPING OUT OF OLE MUDDY

As a member of President John F. Kennedy's Cabinet, Attorney General Robert Kennedy was privy to the secret policy debate in the early 1960s over how and when to send American troops to South Vietnam.

President Kennedy's military commitment to South Vietnam was firmly in place at the time of his assassination in 1963, but whether it would have escalated in the ensuing years to the extent ordered by his successor, President Lyndon Johnson, remains one of the great unanswered questions of the era.

Not subject to conjecture is Robert Kennedy's position on the war.

By the time he announced his candidacy for president in 1967, Robert Kennedy had discarded his earlier support of the war and openly aligned himself with the peace movement. His rejection of Lyndon Johnson's war policy—and his apology for his own role in the development of that policy—was a cornerstone of his candidacy.

Less than a year after his public apology, he was killed by an assassin's bullet. Many Americans, to this day, still believe that there is a conspiratorial link between his apology and his murder.

THE APOLOGY

"I was involved in many of the early decisions on Vietnam, decisions which helped set up our present path. It may be that the effort was doomed from the start, that it was never really possible to bring all the people of South Vietnam under the rule of the successive governments we supported—governments, one after another, riddled with corruption, inefficiency, and greed. . . .

"If that is the case, as it well may be, then I am willing to bear my share of the responsibility, before history and before my fellow citizens. But past error is no excuse for its own perpetuation. Tragedy is a tool for the living to gain wisdom, not as a guide by which to live.

"Now as ever, we do ourselves best justice when we measure ourselves against ancient tests, as in the *Antigone* of Sophocles: 'All men make mistakes, but a good man yields when he knows his course is wrong, and repairs the evil. The only sin is pride.'"[57]

PEARL HARBOR
SNEAK ATTACK BLAMED ON POOR TYPING SKILLS

On December 7, 1941, more than one hundred Japanese warplanes and a number of midget submarines attacked the United States' Pacific fleet at Pearl Harbor, Hawaii. At anchor were nearly ninety ships, including the battleship *Arizona,* which was among the nineteen ships destroyed by the Japanese.

Almost 2,500 American servicemen were killed in the attack, with another eight hundred listed as missing. In the angry days that followed, President Franklin Roosevelt referred to the sneak attack as a day that would "live in infamy."

Without the attack, it is questionable whether the United States would have entered World War II. Because of the attack, Congress ended up issuing a Declaration of War against both Japan and Germany.

Everyone knows how that war ended, of course, but for years many Americans felt something was missing from the peace settlement—an apology.

It took nearly half a century for the Japanese to apologize for Pearl Harbor, and when the apology finally arrived, it wasn't exactly what Americans expected.

In what must be regarded as one of the worst excuses for an apology in history, the Japanese apologized not for the atrocities committed during the sneak attack, but rather for a clerical error that prevented the Japanese embassy in Washington from properly notifying American leaders of the impending action.

The "apology" arrived with an explanation.

According to the Japanese Foreign Ministry, their country's declaration of war was to have been delivered at 1 P.M., twenty-five minutes before the attack began. Instead, the message was delayed by Japan's First Secretary at the embassy, who could not find anyone in the office with the needed security clearance to type the decoded message for delivery to the White House. The First Secretary, a clumsy typist at best, typed it out himself, but by the time he was able to finish, the attack had already begun.

> ## THE APOLOGY
>
> Apologizing for the clumsiness of their embassy personnel, the Japanese Foreign Ministry issued this statement in November 1994: "It is extremely regrettable that such a thing happened, which we consider inexcusable. . . . There were also differences of understanding between the Foreign Ministry and the Japanese embassy there. In that sense, the entire Foreign Ministry was responsible."[58]

JESSE VENTURA
MINNESOTA GOVERNOR TANGLES WITH GOD

It would be an understatement to say that most people were surprised when former professional wrestler Jesse "The Body" Ventura was elected governor of Minnesota in 1998. His supporters called him a breath of fresh air, someone who would "talk straight" to the people.

The media *loved* Ventura. He is a reporter's dream. He's big, he's colorful, he's prone to maverick positions on political and social issues—and, most important, he can be counted on to engage in off-the-wall behavior, such as packing heat when he's out among the common people making his rounds as governor.

There's another reason reporters are infatuated with Ventura: He's living proof that government has reached the point, finally, where it is willing to stand up and admit that it no longer can find any reason to justify its existence.

Ventura's first year as governor was filled with news, most of which was centered on comments he made that, in turn, led to demands for apologies.

Ventura's first gaffe came less than a month after he was sworn in, when he was a guest on *Late Night with David Letterman.* When Let- terman asked him which city he preferred— Minneapolis or St. Paul—the governor chose the former. "Have you ever been to St. Paul?" he asked. "Whoever designed the streets must have been drunk. . . . I think it was those Irish guys, you know what they like to do." With that, he gestured as if he were taking a drink.

Later in the summer, he was caught using salty language at a professional wrestling event, at which scantily clad women paraded about the arena and wrestlers repeatedly slammed plastic tables against one another.

The third big gaffe of 1999 came in the fall, with publication of an interview in *Playboy.* In it Ventura took controversial stands on a variety of issues—he wants to legalize prostitution and drug use—but it was his position on religion that got him in trouble.

"Organized religion is a sham and a crutch for weak-minded people who need strength in numbers," he said in the interview. "It tells people to go stick their noses in other people's business. The religious right wants to tell people how to live."

THE APOLOGY

For his comments about "drunken Irishmen," Ventura said, "If I offended anyone, I apologize—the David Letterman show is a show of comedy. It's a show that has 'Top Ten' lists and it is generally considered comedic, and that's the light in which I did the show, was to go on there and have fun."

For his salty language at the wrestling event, Ventura refused to apologize. He said the press should steer clear of his private activities.

For his comments about religion being a "crutch," Ventura admitted making a mistake and vowed to rein himself in, but he continued to blame the media for reporting his comments. "It's sad, because I get four or five people who come up to me on a daily basis and say, 'Governor, don't change. Be who you've got to be,'" he says. "But in light of my family and self-preservation, I know that I have to change."[59]

RAPE OF NANKING
ANOTHER HORRIFYING CHAPTER OF WORLD WAR II

In November 1937, following their successful invasion of Shanghai, the Japanese war machine set its sights on the Chinese capital of Nanking. The city fell on December 13, setting in motion an orgy of violence seldom seen in human history.

Japanese soldiers rounded up tens of thousands of young men and herded them to the outskirts of the city, where they were used for bayonet practice, soaked with gasoline, and burned alive—or simply shot to death.

Historians estimate that close to 350,000 Chinese were killed.

Also brutalized were between 20,000 and 80,000 Chinese women, who were raped and, in some cases, tortured by Japanese soldiers. The women were nailed alive to walls, their breasts were sliced off, and some of them were disemboweled.

After the war, the atrocities at Nanking were covered up by both the Chinese and the Japanese governments. Not until the 1990s were they finally exposed.

Interviewed for the 1997 book *The Rape of Nanking* by Iris Chang, Hakudo Nagatomi admitted his role in the atrocities. "The Japanese officer proposed a test of my courage," said Nagatomi. "He unsheathed his sword, spat on it, and with a sudden mighty swing he brought it down on the neck of a Chinese boy cowering before us. . . . The officer suggested I take the head home as a souvenir. I remember smiling proudly as I took his sword and began killing people."

THE APOLOGY

Hakudo Nagatomi did more than apologize for his actions in Nanking.

Today a successful doctor in Japan, he built a shrine of remorse in his waiting room. While waiting to see the doctor, patients can watch videotapes of his trial and a full confession of his crimes. For nearly sixty years, Nagatomi has been consumed with remorse.

"I beheaded people, starved them to death, burned them, and buried them alive, over two hundred in all. It is terrible that I could turn into an animal and do these things. There are really no words to explain what I was doing. I was truly a devil."[60]

HENRY CISNEROS

HOUSING SECRETARY BUSTED FOR SEX LIE

When President Bill Clinton appointed him Housing Secretary, former San Antonio, Texas, mayor Henry Cisneros was considered one of the rising stars of the Democratic Party. He was young, gifted, and Hispanic—all definite political pluses.

Like all other high-ranking federal appointees, he was interviewed by the FBI as part of his background check. It was well-known in Texas that Cisneros was having marital problems, and it was even rumored that the main reason he did not run for governor was an extramarital affair with a woman named Linda Jones.

At the time of the FBI interview, he was forthright about his affair, and when asked if he had ever paid her money, he admitted that he had, but he lied about the amount. He swore he had paid her less than $2,500.

When the FBI uncovered evidence that the actual amount was closer to $250,000, federal prosecutors indicted Cisneros on eighteen felony counts, including lying to the FBI. Linda Jones was indicted on charges of conspiracy, bank fraud, money laundering, and obstruction of justice. Cisneros pleaded not guilty.

Jones pleaded guilty to the charges and was sentenced to three and a half years in prison. She was later offered a reduction in her sentence if she agreed to testify as a government witness.

Just as Cisneros's trial was about to begin, he pleaded guilty to a misdemeanor charge of lying to the FBI about payments to Jones. The judge fined him ten thousand dollars but did not impose a prison term or place him on probation.

As a result of the incident, Cisneros left politics and entered the private sector. Today he is president of Univision, a cable network that reaches ninety percent of Hispanic households in the United States. In its October 1999 issue, *Entertainment Weekly* selected him as one of the one hundred most powerful people in the entertainment industry.

THE APOLOGY

Cisneros admitted in court that he lied to the FBI.

"I accept responsibility for the conduct as outlined," he said.

"I know there will be some second-guessing about this plea," said the judge, referring to the leniency of its terms. "There will be some who will say that the sanction is not tough enough and others who will say here is more evidence of the Independent Counsel Act not serving the public trust. . . . [But] we cannot permit an individual to lie his way into high public office. . . . The work of the independent counsel in this case reaffirms the importance of telling the truth."

Later, in a prepared statement given to reporters, Cisneros apologized for his actions: "I regret my lack of candor. . . . I hope that all who follow me in public service learn the lesson that truth and candor are important in the process of selecting our leaders."[61]

TAI COLLINS
MAYBE THE MASSAGE WAS THE MESSAGE

In the summer of 1983, Tai Collins thought she had it all.

At the age of twenty, she was the newly crowned Miss Virginia–USA—and the sought-after companion of Virginia governor Charles Robb. She knew that he was married to ex-President Lyndon Johnson's daughter, Lynda Bird, and she knew that he had three children, but those technicalities paled in comparison to the excitement generated by the governor's telephone calls, flowers, letters, and gifts.

Collins and Robb first met, according to the beauty queen, during a modeling assignment at a Norfolk shopping mall. Robb was there to officiate over a ribbon-cutting ceremony; Collins was there to model white satin and black lace.

After the ceremony, the smitten governor sent Collins a letter at the lingerie store where she worked and then he asked a friend to call her to set up a date. Their affair lasted less than a year, according to Collins, and by the time Robb began his 1987 campaign for the Senate, she had married—and divorced—an East Coast retail executive and was no longer interested in the politics of forsaken love.

The Robb-Collins affair became campaign news when reporters learned of the relationship. One newspaper described their affair with a headline that read CHUCK AND TAI, SEX AND DRUGS! Robb denied the affair but admitted meeting the model in hotel rooms for private "massages." The scandal continued well past Robb's election to the Senate, but then quietly moved off the front pages and into the footnotes of history.

Collins was last seen on the pages of *Playboy*, where she posed nude and talked openly about her affair with Robb.

THE APOLOGY

"I know the whole thing looks bad," said Robb, who was the first to apologize. "Clearly, some of the things that I have done are not appropriate for a middle-aged, happily married man."

Then it was Collins's turn.

"I know I was not supposed to have an affair with a married man, but I'm human, too," she said. "I take responsibility for what I did. I'm a Christian, I go to church on Sunday. Whether God forgives me or I forgive myself—it's not for the public to judge me."[62]

SUPREME COURT OF CANADA
JUSTICE BLUSHES OVER SLIP OF TONGUE

At the Phi Delta Phi fraternity initiation banquet in Toronto, Ontario, Canadian Supreme Court Justice Ian Binnie was reading aloud to the assembled members from the official Phi Delta Phi booklet on rituals, when, suddenly, he came across a portion of the text that struck him as particularly amusing:

"The use of the Fraternity flag, wigs, candles, and dramatic lighting will vary depending on the setting, character, and tradition of the Inn."

It was at that point that the Justice decided to have a little fun at the fraternity's expense. Making reference to the booklet's description of wigs and candles, the Justice told the stunned audience at the Osgoode Hall Law School that the words put him in mind of a "faggoty dress-up party."

The Justice was ill prepared for the uproar that followed.

In a letter to the dean of the Osgoode Hall Law School, Justice Binnie apologized for his use of the phrase "faggoty dress-up party." In his defense, he said he had seen the phrase in a newspaper review of a production of *MacBeth* at the world-renowned Stratford Festival.

Thanks to his prompt and seemingly heartfelt apology, Justice Binnie managed to walk away from the incident with a mere slap on the wrist.

THE APOLOGY

"The expression popped out last Saturday without any reflection on my part about its precise significance," he wrote in his letter, which was subsequently posted on the Internet.

"I don't consider the word 'faggoty' to be appropriate, nor is the pejorative attitude that lies behind it acceptable, nor do I subscribe to it. Sometimes, as here, expressions that stick in your mind lose their original edge and significance with the passage of time. Individuals are deserving of equal consideration and respect, and I certainly regret the fact that what was intended to poke fun at Phi Delta Phi was taken literally by some of the students."

REPRESENTATIVE DICK ARMEY
TEXAN INSERTS FOOT INTO MOUTH

Congressmen Dick Armey of Texas and Barney Frank of Massachusetts sit on opposite sides of the fence. Armey is a conservative, heterosexual Republican. Frank is a liberal, homosexual Democrat. The two men seldom agree on anything.

One of the big stories of 1995 was a book deal signed by Speaker of the House Newt Gingrich. It stood to make him a millionaire.

Republican leaders, such as Armey, felt it necessary to defend the Speaker.

In an interview with radio journalists, ostensibly to discuss the Speaker's book deal, Armey focused his attention on fellow congressman Barney Frank, who had vociferously protested the transaction.

"I like peace and quiet, and I don't need to listen to Barney Fag . . . er . . . Barney Frank haranguing in my ear," Armey said.

Reaction was immediate.

"Representative Armey's comment is deplorable and dangerous," said a spokesperson for the National Gay and Lesbian Task Force. "For a member of the House of Representatives to use such a childish but harmful slur is beneath that office and must be roundly condemned by his colleagues."

Under fire, Armey apologized.

THE APOLOGY

"This is nothing more than the unintentional mispronunciation of another person's name that sounded like something it was not."[63]

THE TATTOOED MAYOR
MICHIGAN OFFICIAL GIVES GIRLS A HELPING HAND

Gerald "Ajax" Ackerman was named "Michigan Public Citizen of the Year" in 1994 in recognition of his inspirational work with troubled youth. He was hailed as a role model for overcoming drugs and alcohol.

Three years later, the tattooed, motorcycle-riding community leader, who liked to wear his hair in a ponytail, was elected mayor of Port Huron, Michigan. By all appearances, he was a model citizen and a hardworking mayor.

But it was what was going on behind the scenes that bothered police. In April 1999, the forty-two-year-old mayor was arrested and charged with twenty-five counts of indecent exposure involving under-aged girls.

According to police records, the mayor exposed himself to little girls between the ages of eight and fifteen. In one instance, said the police, Ackerman ordered three girls, aged nine to thirteen, to remove their clothes and perform oral sex on him.

At his trial, Ackerman denied doing anything inappropriate to any of his accusers. However, he said there was a possibility that four girls might have seen him exposed "accidentally."

A jury convicted him on nine counts of indecent exposure, but they were unable to reach verdicts on sixteen other counts of sexual misconduct. The judge sentenced the former mayor—he had resigned the day after his arrest—to one year in prison.

THE APOLOGY

Before being escorted from court in handcuffs, Ackerman told the judge that he was sorry. "I'm willing to accept my convictions . . . [but] I spent twelve years in this community doing everything I could to contribute. I've helped numerous children in this community over a number of years."[64]

DICK MORRIS
POLITICAL ADVISER SUCKED INTO SEX SCANDAL

For years he was Bill Clinton's secret weapon.

As a hired gun, Dick Morris worked for both Republicans and Democrats, but it was his work for the Clinton presidential campaigns that seemed to provide him with his most spectacular political victories.

Always he worked behind the scenes as a private citizen. It was not until Clinton's 1996 reelection campaign that he assumed a more visible role, receiving more than two hundred thousand dollars in consulting fees and expenses from the president.

By that time, Clinton considered him to be his top political adviser.

All that unraveled in 1996, when a weekly tabloid, the *Star*, ran a front-page story that exposed Morris's year-long relationship with a prostitute named Sherry Rowlands. The story included photos of the couple on the balcony of Morris's hotel suite.

Making matters worse was Rowlands's allegations that Morris had allowed her to eavesdrop on telephone conversations he had with the President. Morris, who was married at the time, resigned shortly after the story was made public.

In the months that followed his resignation, Morris appeared on numerous talk shows to apologize for his actions. It was not until the publication of his book, *Behind the Oval Office*, that he offered a detailed written apology.

THE APOLOGY

"I owe my wife, Eileen, President Clinton, Vice President Gore, and my colleagues in the White House a public apology. What was I thinking? I wasn't thinking."

Morris blamed his attraction to a prostitute on the solitude he felt in Washington.

"Foolishly, I trusted this woman [Rowlands] and even deluded myself to the point of thinking of her as a friend, though like all men who have paid for sex I am guilty of exploiting the woman involved."

Morris readily acknowledged his relationship with a prostitute, but he denied allowing her to eavesdrop on his conversations with the President. All he did, he explained, was hold the phone up to her ear so that she could hear his voice.

"Sometimes one has to lose almost everything to gain the beginning of self-knowledge and truly accept responsibility for one's conduct," he concluded. "It may take a lifetime to repair the damage I have done, but I have learned from my fall and I will try."[65]

JERRY SPRINGER
IT WAS ONE CHECK TOO MANY

Shortly after being elected to the Cincinnati city council in 1969, Jerry Springer celebrated his victory by joining a "health club" across the river in Kentucky. It was actually a whorehouse that operated under the guise of a health club.

Springer made two visits to the so-called health club, paying the prostitute with a personal check. Some time later the club was raided and shut down, and its records were confiscated by the police. The councilman forgot about the matter and moved on to other interests. Five years later, he received an anonymous phone call.

"We know you were at the club," said the caller.

There were no demands for money. No threats. Just a reminder that someone out there knew that Springer—a liberal, Jewish, transplanted New Yorker who had recently gotten married—had visited a house of prostitution and paid for sex with a personal check. However the call was meant, Springer took it as a threat.

Not certain what the caller had in mind, but certain that whatever it was, it would not advance his career in politics, Springer called a press conference and publicly apologized to Cincinnati voters. At the press conference, Jerry Springer told reporters about the prostitute, and he held up the canceled checks he had written to the health club. "Look," he said, "I was there!" Then he announced his resignation and said he was returning to private life to practice law.

He said he was sorry for any embarrassment his actions had caused others.

The following year, he changed his mind and ran for his old seat on the city council. He was reelected. Then, two years later, he ran for mayor and was elected. At the age of thirty-three, he was one of the youngest mayors in the city's history. He wore his youth the way previous mayors had worn their ties to organized labor or big business. He openly courted rock stars, offering them keys to the city.

In 1982, Springer set his sights on an even bigger job, the governor of Ohio. Since Cincinnati voters had accepted his apology for the incident with the prostitute, he thought that it would be in his best interests to revisit the issue. In a paid television advertisement, he again apologized for accepting the services of a prostitute.

Ohio voters figured two apologies were one too many.

Springer was defeated in the primary and left politics to pursue a career in television.[66]

THE APOLOGY

"Nine years ago I spent time with a woman I shouldn't have. And I paid her with a check. I wish I hadn't done that. And the truth is, I wish no one would ever know. But in the rough world of politics, opponents are not about to let personal embarrassments be laid to rest."

Chapter 6

A Sporting Life

TONYA HARDING
CAT FIGHT ENDS IN TELEVISED HISS-OFF

It had been four years since Olympic hopeful Nancy Kerrigan was assaulted at the Lillehammer games by Tonya Harding's ex-husband and two of his buddies. The FBI would later refer to them, in internal memos, as the "Three Stooges."

The image of Kerrigan grabbing her battered knee and wailing, "Why me? Why me?"—her face contorted not just by the physical pain, but by the realization of what it meant to her career—remains one of the unforgettable moments in Olympic history.

Then there was the image of Harding, the dirty-blonde bad girl of skating, wriggling into her pickup truck with a promise to "kick butt" in the Olympics. She knew she would never be America's sweetheart, but, frankly, she didn't seem to give a damn. She wanted to win, that's all.

So there they were four years later, face-to-face in a Fox Television studio on the eve of the 1998 Winter Olympics. Each had been paid $100,000 simply to show up for the interview. Kerrigan clearly wanted an apology. Harding, who always felt she was the better skater, wanted to outmaneuver her rival in front of millions.

If Fox executives thought the two women would hug and cry in front of the cameras, with Harding spewing forth heartfelt apologies and Kerrigan embracing her rival with the grace of an American Sweetheart, granting forgiveness on the spot, they were dead wrong.

Just before Tonya Harding entered the room, the Fox interviewer asked Nancy Kerrigan what she thought of her former rival. "I don't regard her," she answered coldly. "I only think about it when asked."

When Harding entered the room, Kerrigan looked sick to her stomach.

"Hello," she said, the "o" seemingly caked with ice.

Playing to the cameras, Harding tried her best to be cheerful.

That was not the image Kerrigan wanted to see. The more Harding talked, the more Kerrigan seemed to retreat within herself. She was clearly uncomfortable.

Then came the apology—or was it?

Kerrigan didn't take the bait. "From all of this, I hope she could learn from that and better her life and not hurt anyone else," she said.[67]

THE APOLOGY

"I would like to apologize again for being in the wrong place at the wrong time and with the wrong people," said Harding, downplaying her own involvement in the incident. "If I would have known, I would have done anything I could to stop it. I say that from the bottom of my heart."

EUGENE ROBINSON

FALCONS PLAYER BUSTED DURING PRE-GAME EVENT

The night before the 1999 Super Bowl game, which pitted the Atlanta Falcons against the Denver Broncos, Falcons defensive safety Eugene Robinson went for a ride in his car. It was the biggest game of his career, and he wanted to relax.

That morning he had been honored by the religious group Athletes in Action. At the breakfast, the million-dollar-a-year player was awarded the 1999 Bart Starr Award, which honors athletes of high moral character.

That was how football fans thought of Robinson, as a man of deep religious faith. While playing for the Seattle Seahawks, he was four times chosen "Man of the Year" for his work with Boys and Girls Clubs, and for his devotion to the Union Gospel Mission, where he worked with people who have cerebral palsy.

What was going through Robinson's head that night in Miami as he drove up and down streets frequented by prostitutes and drug dealers, only he knows for certain. According to police records, he approached a female undercover officer for the Miami police at about 9 P.M. and offered her forty dollars for oral sex. Robinson was busted on the spot for solicitation and taken off to jail.

Two hours later, he was released into the custody of Falcons general manager Harold Richardson after signing a promise to appear in court within thirty days. The next day, after a sleepless night, he was a starter for Super Bowl XXXIII, which Atlanta lost to Denver by a score of 34–19. After the game, Robinson apologized to his team and family.

NFL spokesman Greg Aiello said the league had no comment. Atlanta Falcons coach Dan Reeves said it was a "family" matter: "I love Eugene unconditionally."

Three months later, despite his proclamation of innocence, Robinson's attorney made a deal with the judge: The charges would be dropped if Robinson submitted to an AIDS test and completed an AIDS awareness course.

THE APOLOGY

"I really believe, and strongly believe, that I will be found innocent of this. What I really want to do now is apologize first to my Lord, Jesus Christ, secondly to my wife and kids, and thirdly to my teammates and the entire NFL organization for the distraction that I may have caused them.

"I regret I was not maintaining the standards I set for myself. I will have to begin shortly, to make amends to everyone who knows me. I want to thank all the people . . . a lot of the football players, a lot of the fans, and particularly my family, who supported and prayed for me at this very, very low point."[68]

JOHN ROCKER

ZANY ATLANTA BRAVES PITCHER STRIKES OUT

Never popular with New York Mets fans, Atlanta Braves relief pitcher John Rocker is usually greeted with boos and jeers whenever he runs toward the mound in Shea Stadium. One reason for that is his aggressive, take-no-prisoners style of pitching. Another reason is his defiant body language and squared-jaw demeanor, which give him a larger-than-life—some would say cartoonlike—appearance on the field.

Rocker seemed to take the verbal abuse on the chin.

Then, in December 1999, *Sports Illustrated* published an interview with Rocker in which he vented his anger at everyone from the New York fans to the Braves organization. He told the magazine writer that he would retire before ever playing for a New York team. Said Rocker: "Imagine having to take the [No.] 7 train to [Shea Stadium] looking like you're [in] Beirut next to some kids with purple hair, next to some queer with AIDS, right next to some dude who got out of jail for the fourth time, right next to some 20-year-old mom with four kids. It's depressing."

Feeling he was on a roll, he continued: "The biggest thing I don't like about New York are the foreigners. You can walk an entire block in Times Square and not hear anybody speaking English. . . . How the hell did they get in this country?"

If Rocker thought the boos from fans at Shea Stadium were obnoxious, then he must have been floored by the nationwide uproar his comments caused. Baseball Commissioner Bud Selig called Rocker's comments "inappropriate and offensive." Braves general manager John Schuerholz said that Rocker's comments "in no way reflect the views of the Atlanta Braves organization."

As a result, Rocker was fined $20,000 (it was later reduced to $500) and banned from all 45 days of spring training and the first 28 days of the 2000 season (the suspension was later reduced to 14 days).

By June 2000, the contorversy appeared to have died down, only to return to the front burner when Rocker confronted the *Sports Illustrated* reporter who wrote the original story that got him in so much hot water. In front of witnesses, Rocker shouted at the reporter and voiced apparent threats against him.

By then, the Atlanta Braves management had had enough. Within days, Rocker was kicked off the team and exiled to the Braves's farm team in Richmond, Virginia. A week later, Rocker was summoned back to Atlanta to replace Rudy Seanez on the roster after the reliever complained of tightness in his right arm.

Stay tuned. There's sure to be more.

THE APOLOGY

"Even though it might appear otherwise from what I've said, I am not a racist. I should not have said what I did, because it is not what I believe in my heart. . . . I want everybody to understand that my emotions fuel my competitive desire. They are a source of energy for me. However, I have let my emotions get the best of my judgment."[69]

MARV ALBERT
MÉNAGE À TROIS SIDELINES SPORTSCASTER

For thirty years he had pursued his dream as a sportscaster. Finally, after years of journeyman labor, he elbowed his way to the top with his trademark call of "Yesss!" and frequent appearances on David Letterman's late-night television show.

America considered Marv Albert to be as much a star as the NBA players upon whom he reported. He was easily the most famous sportscaster on television.

Then came news in 1997 that he had been arrested in Virginia and charged with forcible sodomy. Albert said he was innocent, that the charges had been trumped up by a longtime lover—and America was willing to believe him.

However, much of that support dwindled during the trial, once the prosecution presented its case that Albert had attacked his lover, bitten her viciously on her back, and forced her to perform oral sex—all because she had not brought along a male sex partner to participate in a ménage à trois.

If all that were not bad enough, along came testimony that Albert liked to wear ladies' underwear, that he wore a wig (one witness said she pulled it off during a struggle in which he was wearing panties and a garter belt), that he had lied about his age on his job application with NBC Sports (he was two years older than he stated), and that he was not even really Marv Albert (his real name being Marvin Aufrichtig).

Albert proclaimed his innocence, right up until the moment he pleaded guilty.

Forcible sodomy was bad enough, but when ladies' panties and allegations of kinky sex with another man entered the picture, NBC Sports, which had stood by Albert throughout the ordeal, told its star sportscaster to take a powder.

As part of a plea-bargain arrangement, Marv Albert pleaded guilty to lesser charges of assault and battery. "Are you pleading guilty to this crime because you are, in fact, guilty of this crime?" asked the judge.

"Yes," answered Albert.

Standing before microphones outside the courtroom, Albert offered not so much an apology as an explanation. "I just felt that I had to end this ordeal for myself, my wonderful family, my fiancée, Heather, my friends, and supporters."

"But what about the panties?" shouted a reporter.

Albert declined to comment.

THE APOLOGY

Not until after he learned he had been fired by NBC Sports—and later accepted a job on New York's MSG cable network as a sports announcer—did he offer a public apology. It was not offered with a brazen vocal flourish, such as he liked to do with his call of "Yesss!", but rather with something of a whimper.

"What I did was wrong," said Albert quietly.[70]

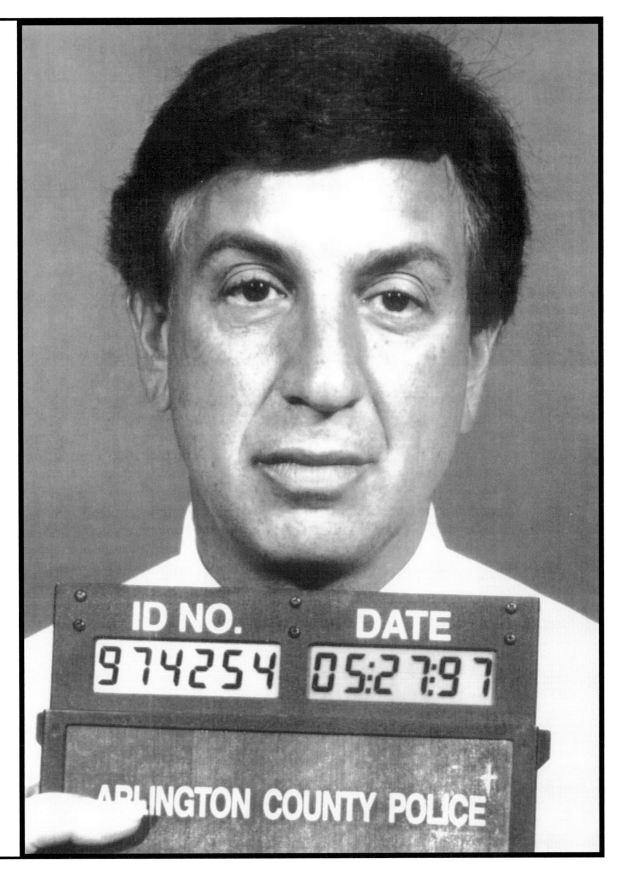

ID NO. 974254 DATE 05:27:97

ARLINGTON COUNTY POLICE

FRANK GIFFORD
KATHIE LEE'S HIGH-FLYING HUBBY SHOT DOWN

Former New York Giants running back Frank Gifford took some punishing shots during his ten-year career in the National Football League in the 1950s and early 1960s. He once took a hit so devastating that he had to sit out an entire season to recover.

However, nothing he ever experienced in the NFL—or later as a television sportscaster—prepared him for the punishment he would undergo as the husband of television personality Kathie Lee Gifford of *Regis & Kathie Lee* fame.

Well, actually it wasn't the marriage that caused him grief, it was his betrayal of that marriage with an airline attendant named Suzen Johnson.

The two first met on a 1993 flight, but it was not until four years later that they succumbed to a two-day tryst. Unknown to Gifford, Johnson had cooperated with a tabloid in a plan to videotape the encounter.

Imagine Gifford's surprise when he and Johnson made the tabloid's cover.

Just when he thought the situation could not possibly get worse, snippets of the videotape were released. "I wanted to do this since I met you," Gifford said in the videotaped conversation with Johnson. "You're so perky."

In the ensuing months, Gifford made various apologies for the incident. In some ways, he said, his infidelity had made his marriage "much stronger."

While a guest on Larry King's live CNN television program, Gifford was asked if he felt any bitterness toward anyone over the incident.

THE APOLOGY

"I was angry for a while, but I got over that. I think we'll know that their time will come [those who set up the video trap]. . . . It isn't for me to be one who judges. All I know is I judge myself, and I was very foolish. I was stupid.

"Fortunately, I was married to a wonderful woman who knew that she was commanded to forgive me. . . . Because of this I really found the God I thought I knew. What happened to me was . . . [a] spiritual experience that made me stronger."[71]

KERRY COLLINS

SAINTS QUARTERBACK SACKED BY DEMON RUM

The Carolina Panthers thought they had a winner when they picked quarterback Kerry Collins as their first-round draft choice in 1995. But, after a couple of seasons, it had become apparent that things weren't working out.

Collins went to the coach and told him his heart just wasn't in the game.

As a result, the quarterback was cut from the roster. Watching this from the sidelines was New Orleans Saints coach Mike Ditka, whose team that year (1998) was ranked twenty-third in the National Football League.

Ditka took a chance on Collins and claimed him off waivers. People said the coach was crazy, but when he took a look at his team—Julian Pittman was in jail in Florida for parole violations; wide receiver Keith Poole had been charged with assaulting a man with a golf club; Joe Johnson, Eric Guliford, and Keno Hills had had their own scrapes with the law—it didn't seem like all that big a risk.

"Our goal is to get better players and be a better team," he explained to reporters. "Sometimes better players aren't better people."

The first year that Collins wore the Saints jersey, the team traveled to North Carolina to play his old team, the Panthers. Collins never got in the game and was constantly booed by the Carolina fans.

Several hours after the game—the Saints were soundly beaten by the Panthers—Collins was arrested by North Carolina police and charged with drunken driving. Told about the incident by reporters, Ditka said, "The last thing I told him was, 'It's a very hostile environment there. Can you handle that?'"

Collins apologized profusely for the incident.

Sometimes apologies work. Sometimes they don't. Collins was subsequently cut from the Saints' roster in February 1999, without an apology, by Coach Ditka.

> ## THE APOLOGY
>
> "I want to publicly apologize to Tom Benson and the entire Saints organization for my behavior, the embarrassment I brought to this organization. I would especially like to apologize to my teammates and coach for the incident and the distraction it has caused. My behavior was totally and completely unacceptable. My behavior was extremely careless and immature and was nothing short of a severe lack of judgment."
>
> Collins denied he had a drinking problem.
>
> "This is my first offense," he said. "It will be my only offense. . . . I realize I'm at a critical junction in my career. Therefore, I'm going to rededicate myself to football."[72]

TIC PRICE

BASKETBALL COACH SLAM-DUNKED BY COED

University of Memphis basketball coach Tic Price was well liked by students and athletes alike. Perhaps a little too well liked.

For about a year, Coach Price, who is married, had an affair with a coed.

The affair came to light in 1999, when Germantown police (Germantown is a suburb of Memphis) received a series of anonymous faxes about the coach. One said the coed had been seen running from Price's home, bleeding.

Police investigated the alleged assault, but did not press charges because the coed refused to talk to them and declined to file a complaint against the coach.

In late 1999, Coach Price held a press conference and—with his wife, Jamie, at his side—resigned his $400,000-a-year position with the university. He cited his extramarital affair as the reason for his resignation.

THE APOLOGY

"I am sorry I let everybody down. I humbly ask for your forgiveness. I will not go into the sordid details of this relationship, but I admit I had an affair. . . . I have hurt my wife deeply and I'm a very lucky man to have her standing by my side today."[73]

CHIPPER JONES
ALL-STAR PLAYER NOT WELL SERVED BY HOOTERS

With a name like "Chipper," you are given bonus points from the get-go.

If you can't trust a man named Chipper, whom can you trust? That is what fans of one of the Atlanta Braves' most popular players of the late 1990s told themselves. For years their hero, Chipper Jones, was held up as a role model for youngsters everywhere.

No other Braves player ever received the ovation he did, both in Atlanta and on the road, according to sports writers who follow the team. Off the field, the all-star third baseman was a spokesman for the Braves' Big League Lunch Program. He was the person fans wanted their sons, brothers, and fathers to be like. What the fans didn't know was that Jones led a double life.

His troubles began in March 1997, when he met a waitress at a West Palm Beach Hooters restaurant that would change his life. Although married, he began a secret affair with the waitress that resulted in a pregnancy. The woman returned to her home state of Michigan to have the baby.

Once the story broke, Jones pledged to support the child.

Jones wasted no time in apologizing for his adulterous affair.

Saying he no longer wanted to be the person he had been for the first five years of his major league career, he said he had done all the "right" things as far as the team was concerned but he had been leading a "hypocritical life."

Interviewed by reporters after her husband's public apology, Karin said she almost did not forgive him. "I got down on my knees, fought with God, went to counselors, called my friends in the wee hours of the morning, and went through a severe depression about leaving for good."

Within a year of the apology, Chipper and Karin filed for divorce.

THE APOLOGY

"I've messed up royally. I've messed up just about as bad as a man can mess up without killing somebody. I've committed adultery, and I'll pay for that for the rest of my life. I want to take this opportunity to publicly apologize to my wife, to the fans, and to the Braves organization for not representing myself very well and not doing the things all those people expect me to. I ask for forgiveness."

Jones said that the day he told his wife, Karin, about the affair was one of the worst days of his life. "It was terrible," he said. "I never want to come close to having to go through that situation again. Just seeing how much pain I can inflict on another human being without putting my hands on them is just unbelievable. I'll never do it again."[74]

ARMANDO BENITEZ
ORIOLES PITCHER AGONIZES OVER BEAN BALL

Baltimore Orioles relief pitcher Armando Benitez was on the mound during a 1998 game with the New York Yankees. The batter was Tino Martinez, who had a batting average of .291, respectable but not great.

Despite his middle-of-the-road batting average, Martinez was the home-run leader of the Yankees, having hit forty-four balls out of the park in 1997. With stats like that, he didn't *need* a high batting average.

Facing Martinez that day, Benitez knew the game was on the line. Benitez had just given up a home run to Bernie Williams that put the Yankees ahead. Who could blame Benitez for being anxious?

Only Benitez knows what pitch he meant to throw. What arrived at home plate was a beanball that struck Martinez in the back. With that, both dugouts emptied as players from both teams engaged in an old-fashioned brawl right there on the field.

Five players, including Benitez, were ejected from the game. The Yankees ended up beating the Orioles by a score of 9–5, handing Baltimore its sixth straight defeat.

The day following the beanball incident, the Orioles were scheduled for a game with the Oakland A's. Before the game, Benitez apologized to his teammates, calling the incident "an embarrassment to the team."

Benitez said he did not intend to hit Martinez and threw a pitch that was meant to go inside. Benitez then ended up with the New York Mets and was thus embraced by another breed of New Yorker—the Mets fan.

THE APOLOGY

"I feel like it's all my fault. I appreciate all the guys talking to me, saying, 'It's not your fault. There's nothing you can do about it. You've got to forget this and help the team.' I'm concerned. Everybody here loves me."

Benitez said he planned to send Martinez a letter of apology.[75]

TIM JOHNSON
MANAGER TELLS ONE STORY TOO MANY

Toronto Blue Jays manager Tim Johnson used a secret weapon to motivate his players: He told inspiring stories about his combat service in Vietnam.

It always seemed to work.

Then, toward the end of the 1998 season, the truth came out. Although Johnson had spent six years with the United States Marine Corps, he served in the reserves and never once went to Vietnam. His entire military experience was spent teaching mortar technology to troops headed to Vietnam. Everything he told his players had been a lie.

Faced with evidence of his falsehoods, Johnson made a public apology.

At a press conference, Johnson said he had apologized to his players and was undergoing therapy. Johnson said he had seen no evidence that the incident has affected his players' performances. "They have all been supportive and said, 'Hey, you showed me something,'" he said. "It was a problem, but I am trying to deal with it and move on."

THE APOLOGY

"It's like somebody has taken a 50,000-pound weight off my shoulders. I've had thirty years of guilt lifted off my back."

Johnson offered an explanation for his lies.

"Friends of mine were going to Vietnam when I was going to spring training," he said. "While they were off fighting and getting killed, I was playing baseball. I've dealt with the guilt for thirty years."[76]

CHRIS CANTY
DOZING CORNERBACK DRAWS PENALTY

The second-year cornerback for the New England Patriots was sitting in a parked car at a gas station in North Attleboro, Massachusetts, when he dozed off while waiting for a friend to arrive.

Spotting the car, police looked inside and saw an open beer container. Chris Canty was awakened and arrested on the spot. He passed a sobriety test, but a check of his license turned up an unpaid speeding ticket. Police also noticed that his car was missing an inspection sticker.

After being charged with driving with an open container in his car, driving with a suspended license, failing to present a license, and failing to have a current vehicle inspection sticker, Canty was released on his own recognizance.

Canty had more at stake than the possibility of jail time.

A first-round, twenty-ninth pick in the college draft two years earlier, Canty had made several high-profile mistakes on the playing field during his first year as a starter, including poor pass coverage that led to a touchdown that gave division rivals the New York Jets a victory. Career-wise, it was not a good time to have a run-in with the law.

After his initial court date, he met with reporters and issued an apology.

THE APOLOGY

"It was definitely a bad judgment call on my part and something that will never happen again. If you do something wrong, you've got to 'fess up."[77]

CHARLES BARKLEY
"YOU CAN LAY THERE AND DIE"

Houston Rockets basketball star Charles Barkley was sitting in an Orlando bar with three women when a man approached his table and tossed a glass of ice at him. Barkley chased the twenty-year-old man to the front of the bar, where an off-duty police officer attempted to intervene in the ensuing scuffle.

Barkley ignored the officer, picked the man up, and threw him through the glass window. The mercurial basketball star then went outside and, as the man lay bleeding on the ground, told him, "You got what you deserve. You don't respect me. I hope you're hurt." Police separated the two men, but Barkley returned and told the man, according to the police report, "For all I care, you can lie there and die."

Barkley was arrested and charged with aggravated battery and resisting arrest without violence. He was held in the Orlando jail for five hours before being released on six thousand dollars bond.

Later that night, Barkley was ejected from the Rockets' exhibition game with the Orlando Magic when he tossed a ball into the stands.

Eight months later, in June 1998, Barkley accepted a plea-bargain agreement that settled the charges against him. One condition of the agreement was that he issue a public apology.

Barkley apologized to the police, but not to the man he tossed out the window. Later in the year, a jury rejected a $550,000 lawsuit against Barkley from the man.

THE APOLOGY

"I greatly regret my involvement in the series of events which occurred . . . in Orlando. The Orlando police officers acted appropriately, and I regret the way I handled my contact with the Orlando police officers that night. . . . I had allowed myself to be provoked by a malicious bar patron, and I realize in hindsight that I compounded the problem by not being initially more cooperative with the officers present. . . . I have always had and will continue to have great respect for law enforcement officers and for the crucial job that they do."[78]

MIKE TYSON
ANOTHER ONE BITES THE DUST

Two years out of prison, where he did time for a rape conviction, former heavyweight boxing champion Mike Tyson attempted to redeem his career—and his personal reputation—with a championship match with Evander Holyfield.

Tyson still had the fearsome look, the wild-eyed glare that seemed born of some primeval passion conjured up in a swamp somewhere, and his pumped-up, thirty-year-old body appeared solid as a rock, but there was something about Tyson the man that disturbed sportswriters. They couldn't put their finger on it, but it was there, lurking in the shadows. No one knew what to expect.

Holyfield had beaten Tyson before, but this fight was about more than simply boxing. Tyson was the meanest boxer who ever lived. Holyfield wasn't as mean, but he was every bit as big— and something else: He was a smarter fighter.

Two rounds into the fight, it became clear that Holyfield was going to win. He was out-boxing Tyson, not overpowering him, just out-punching him. Faced with that probability, Tyson suddenly snapped.

While the two men were in a clinch, Tyson leaned over and took a bite out of Holyfield's ear. Still the fight continued. Then Tyson did it again, biting off a crescent portion of Holyfield's ear, which he spat into the ring. With that, the fight was immediately stopped by the referee, with Holyfield declared the winner.

After the fight, Tyson blamed the incident on Holyfield. He said he bit Holyfield's ear because the fighter had head-butted him in the ring. Head butting, in Tyson's view, was every bit as bad as ear biting.

Holyfield's explanation seemed to make more sense: "He wasn't up for another beating. He realized he couldn't whup me, and he got frustrated."

Tyson left the ring that night a loser in ways he never fully understood.

Two days after the fight, Mike Tyson held a press conference.

THE APOLOGY
(Part I)

"I'm here to apologize today to the people that expect more of Mike Tyson, to forgive me for snapping in the ring, and doing something that I've never done before, and will never do again.

"Evander, I am sorry. You're a champion and I respect that, and I'm only saddened that the fight didn't go on further so that the boxing fans of the world might have seen for themselves who would come out on top."

As apologies go, it wasn't a very good one.

The following week, while standing before the Nevada Athletic Commission, which had the authority to suspend his boxing license, Tyson was prodded to try another apology. Sullenly repentant, Tyson offered a sweeping apology to the Commission.

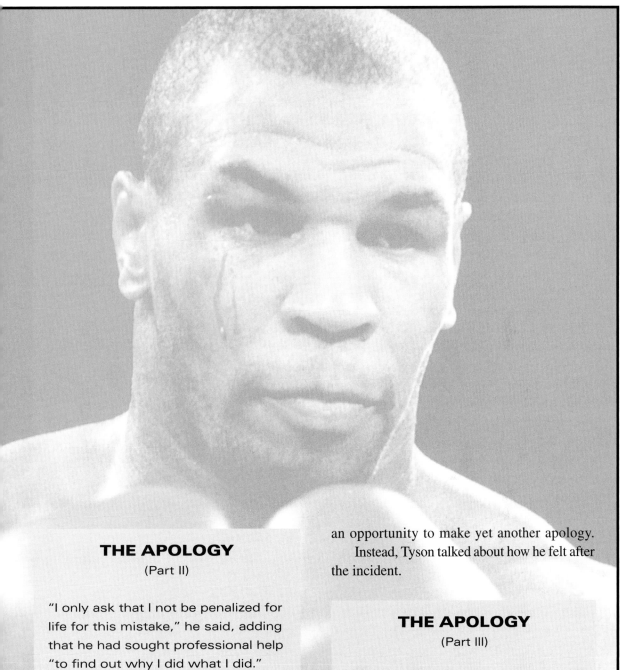

THE APOLOGY
(Part II)

"I only ask that I not be penalized for life for this mistake," he said, adding that he had sought professional help "to find out why I did what I did."

The Commission did not ban him from boxing, but it temporarily suspended his license.

In 1998, while trying to get his license reinstated, Tyson sat down for an interview with *Playboy*. The interviewer asked him about the incident with Holyfield and gave the fighter an opportunity to make yet another apology. Instead, Tyson talked about how he felt after the incident.

THE APOLOGY
(Part III)

"I felt all messed up. . . . I didn't feel too cool about it. But it was over and I had to deal with it. . . . I was never angry before in a fight. So I was embarrassed. I was shocked, scared, I didn't want to do that to him. I'd rather have him beat me."[79]

DENNIS RODMAN
WORM BURROWS INTO MORMON NEST

On the basketball court he has head-butted an official, punched an opponent in the groin, and kicked a cameraman. Off the court . . . well, for the most part, the public has been spared the gritty details of Dennis Rodman's embarrassing off-court antics.

Unfortunately, one or two occasionally slip through the net.

In 1997 Rodman accompanied his team, the Chicago Bulls, to Salt Lake City, Utah, for the NBA finals, where the Bulls were pitted against the Utah Jazz.

Asked by a reporter why his performance did not seem to be up to par at the finals, Rodman first blamed it on a lack of sex. Then he blamed it on Salt Lake City. "It's difficult to get [into] sync here," said Rodman, according to CBS Sportsline. "You know, you've got a bunch of asshole Mormons out here. You can quote me on that."

Bulls coach Phil Jackson defended his aging player: "He may not even know it's a religious cult or sect or whatever it is. . . . We're not concerned about that, we're concerned about his play on the court." But NBA deputy commissioner Russ Granks called Rodman's comments "obviously offensive and inexcusable."

Before the series of games were completed, it became apparent that an apology was in order. It was offered on the Bulls' practice court as the team prepared for game six in the series with the Jazz.

THE APOLOGY

"Like I said, I would have said it if we were in Houston or anything else. But if I knew it was like a religious-type deal, I would have never said it. I'm sorry about that."

In true Rodman fashion, he then blamed it on the fans.

"The people were giving me the finger and things like that," he said. "As far as people who go to games and give me the finger, I think that's wrong, too. They call me a lot of names, the people in the stands. As far as the religion, I have no business saying anything like that, so I take that statement back."[80]

FUZZY ZOELLER

GOLFER MAKES BIGGEST BOGEY OF CAREER

For years, Fuzzy Zoeller was one of the most popular players on the PGA Tour. Fans of the sport liked him. Other golfers liked him. He always attracted lots of media attention, primarily because of his easygoing personality and his willingness to toss a colorful phrase or two in the direction of quote-hungry sportswriters.

Then along came Tiger Woods.

The first tournament Woods entered as a professional, he won. Two weeks later, he delighted spectators at the Phoenix Open with a hole-in-one. Then, in April 1997, he entered his first major tournament, the Masters. To the amazement of the older players competing against him—Woods was only twenty-one—he breezed through the course, dazzling players and spectators with his skill.

Among Woods's competitors at the Masters was forty-five-year-old Zoeller, who simply could not keep up with the younger player. On the final day of the contest, which Woods won handily, Zoeller gave an interview to CNN, which was not broadcast until several days later.

"That little boy is driving well and he's putting well," Zoeller said in the interview, referring to Woods, who also had attracted attention for his age and his African-American heritage. "He's doing everything it takes to win. So you know what you guys do when he gets here? You pat him on the back and say 'Congratulations' and 'Enjoy it,' and tell him not to serve fried chicken next year. Got it?"

Zoeller snapped his fingers and turned to walk away, pausing just long enough to toss one more grenade over his shoulder: "Or collard greens or whatever the hell they serve."

Tiger Woods told reporters he was stunned by Zoeller's racially tinged remarks, but did not feel that the offending comments were intentional. He said he had played golf with Zoeller on other occasions and had found him to be a "jokester."

Equally stunned was Zoeller, who suddenly found himself under attack from the same public that had laughed at his jokes so many times in the past. The golfer withdrew from the Greater Greensboro Chrysler Classic and told reporters he wanted to talk to Woods about his remarks before picking up another golf club.

THE APOLOGY

"I am the one who screwed up, and I will pay the price. I started this, and I feel strongly that I have to make things right with Tiger first before anything else. I also regret the distraction this has caused the world of golf. What I said is distracting people at this tournament."

Later, Woods told reporters he accepted Zoeller's apology.[81]

Chapter 7

Forgive Me, O Lord

SOUTHERN BAPTIST CONVENTION

LET'S FORGET ABOUT THAT SLAVERY THING, OKAY?

The Southern Baptist Convention was founded in Augusta, Georgia, in 1845, in retaliation against northern Baptist abolitionists who refused to allow southern Baptists to serve as missionaries because of their support of slavery.

Since missionary work is one of the building blocks of the faith, the southerners felt they had no choice but to bolt the church and establish their own denomination.

Each year since its creation, the convention has met to take care of the business of its thirty-nine thousand member churches, which include nearly two thousand black congregations. Not since well before the Civil War had the subject of slavery arisen.

Inexplicably, at the 1995 convention a resolution was introduced that required the church to issue an apology for its past positions on slavery. It also called for members to repent for lingering vestiges of racism.

To everyone's surprise, the resolution was approved by a show of hands at the convention, attended by more than fifteen thousand voting clergy and laypeople. It proved to be the largest mass expression of regret for past wrongs in modern history.

Later, at a press conference, the Rev. Jim Henry, president of the Southern Baptist Convention, described the apology as "one of our finest moments."

THE APOLOGY

"We apologize to all African Americans for condoning and/or perpetuating individual and systemic racism in our lifetime, and we genuinely repent of racism of which we have been guilty, whether consciously or unconsciously," said the resolution, which went on to ask forgiveness from African Americans.

The purpose of such an apology, said the resolution, was to "repudiate historic acts of evil, such as slavery, from which we continue to reap a bitter harvest."[82]

POPE JOHN PAUL II
PONTIFF ASKS FORGIVENESS FOR WRONGS OF CATHOLICS

For weeks leading up to Pope John Paul II's March 2000 homily for the Day of Pardon Mass in St. Peter's Basilica in Vatican City, rumors circulated that the Pontiff was going to apologize for centuries of wrongs committed by Catholics.

Wild speculation abounded in the media.

When the time came for the homily, Pope John Paul II lived up to the advance billing and cited the use of violence "in the service of the truth" and hostility toward followers of other religions as reasons for the church to examine its collective conscience.

Although the Pontiff did not name names during his address, observers surmised that his comments were meant to address three historical blemishes on the church: the burning of heretics at the stake during the Inquisition, the slaughter of Muslims during the Crusades, and the silence of many Catholics during the Nazi Holocaust of World War II. During the homily, one of the cardinals in attendance did specify the need for a divine pardon for offenses that contributed to the "sufferings of the people of Israel."

It was an unprecedented moment in the history of the Catholic Church.

THE APOLOGY

"We are deeply saddened by the behavior of those who in the course of history have caused these children of yours to suffer, and asking your forgiveness we wish to commit ourselves to genuine brotherhood. . . . We are asking pardon for the divisions among Christians, for the use of violence that some have committed in the service of truth, and for attitudes of mistrust and hostility assumed toward followers of other religions. . . . We forgive, and we ask forgiveness."[83]

FATHER EDWARD McKEOWN
EX-PRIEST PLEADS GUILTY TO TAKING ADVANTAGE OF YOUNG BOYS

For twenty years, Father Edward McKeown served in parishes across Tennessee, often working with children. In addition to his duties as a schoolteacher in the Nashville Diocese, he directed Catholic youth organizations and later, after his 1989 retirement as a priest, he worked for the Davidson County juvenile court in Nashville.

Unknown to parishioners, McKeown used his authority as a teacher and priest to get close to children he molested and raped during that twenty-year period. In June 1999, McKeown pleaded guilty to molesting and raping a Nashville youth. Police said he was responsible for about thirty additional sexual assaults.

McKeown admitted giving his victims alcohol and marijuana "in order to take advantage of them and make them more easily coerced," said Helen Donnelly, the assistant district attorney general who prosecuted the ex-priest.

At his sentencing, McKeown stood before the judge, his ankles chained together at the cuffs of his prisoner's jumpsuit. The judge showed little compassion and gave McKeown a 25-year prison sentence. As he left the courtroom, McKeown refused to look at his victim, who was seated only a few feet away.

THE APOLOGY

McKeown made no public apology. Rather, he left that to his attorney, Richard McGee, and Bishop Edward Kmiec of the Nashville Diocese.

"He's very sorry," McKeown's attorney told reporters. "He pleaded guilty because he didn't want to put this young man through any more pain. If that meant he spends more time in prison than he might have received with a trial, he was prepared to do that. . . . He would rather die in prison than put him through a trial."

In a written statement that was read at Mass at Catholic churches throughout Nashville, the bishop asked for forgiveness "in the name of the Church for the evil perpetrated by some of its priests."[84]

JIMMY SWAGGART
THE DEVIL MADE HIM DO IT

Jimmy Swaggart had everything a Southern preacher could want.

His $140 million-a-year Assemblies of God ministry, whose headquarters are located on the outskirts of Baton Rouge, Louisiana, in a massive, 7,500-seat complex named the Family Worship Center, reached millions of viewers in more than 120 nations.

Swaggart was revered by a nation of Pentecostal true-believers known derisively as "Holy Rollers" by their upper-crust Protestant cousins. The fact that he was kin to Southern music royalty (rock 'n' roller Jerry Lee Lewis is his first cousin) only elevated his reputation among the faithful.

The Holy Man was well on his way to a higher level of Super Preacherdom—until that fateful day in 1986 when he stumbled and fell into the arms of a prostitute named Debra Murphree. That fall from grace might well have remained the secret of the Holy Man, Debra the Prostitute, and the Lord himself had not the police intervened.

Swaggart's arrest for solicitation of a prostitute made national, front-page headlines. His congregation was stunned.

The Assemblies of God ordered Swaggart suspended for one year, but the Holy Man just couldn't see his way to comply. It is difficult enough for a sinner to find God in a troubled world, but that struggle is nothing compared to the difficulty of giving up a multimillion-dollar fortune.

The Holy Man fought like hell.

The battle seemed to be going his way until Debra the Prostitute reenacted for *Penthouse* magazine the poses she had assumed with the Holy Man. The magazine sold out in five days.

Swaggart fought hard for his ministry—and his millions—for more than a year. Then, on February 21, 1988, he went before his dwindling congregation and begged for their forgiveness, offering a television apology that was as spellbinding as it was creepy.

THE APOLOGY

"I do not plan in any way to whitewash my sin," Swaggart told his followers, his clean-shaven face contorted with the lines of rampant grief and his brow flowing with rivers of sweat. "I do not call it a mistake, a mendacity. I call it sin."

One by one, he apologized to those he had hurt—his wife, his son, his daughter-in-law, the Assemblies of God who had brought the gospel to him when his family was "lost without Jesus."

Finally, he apologized to Jesus himself, "the one who has saved me and washed me and cleansed me." With his cheeks bathed in tears and his swollen eyes uplifted, he professed in a trembling voice: "I have sinned against you, my Lord, and I would ask that your precious blood would wash and cleanse every stain until it is in the seas of God's forgetfulness, never to be remembered against me."[85]

Chapter 8

"I'm Sorry—But I Didn't Do It"

SENATOR BOB PACKWOOD
SEXUAL HARASSMENT CHARGES END CAREER

Within the Republican Party, Bob Packwood was known as something of a maverick, in that early in his career he supported abortion rights, United States aid to Israel, and reform of the tax laws—positions not dear to the heart of the GOP.

Ever since entering the Senate in 1969, he aligned himself with issues important to female voters back home in his native Oregon. Imagine everyone's surprise when several women alleged in 1992 that the senator had made unwanted sexual advances toward them.

The charges were so serious that the Senate Ethics Panel felt compelled to conduct an investigation. By the time its work was completed in 1995, nineteen women had come forward and charged Packwood with sexual misconduct.

By a unanimous vote, the panel recommended his expulsion from the Senate.

Four months later, Packwood announced his resignation.

Standing on the floor of the Senate, Packwood wept as he recounted his years in the chamber.

THE ANTI-APOLOGY

"It is my duty to resign. It is the honorable thing to do for this country, for this Senate. . . . I leave this institution with no malice but with love."

Later, Packwood was asked by reporters if he was sorry.

"Am I sorry?" he asked rhetorically. "Of course—if I did the things they said I did."[86]

JIM BAKKER

TV EVANGELIST DIRTY-DANCES WITH THE DEVIL

Jim and Tammy Faye Bakker were the King and Queen of television evangelism. For a time, their PTL Ministries broadcast one of the most popular syndicated shows on television. Jim with his earnest, smiling face, and Tammy Faye with her oversized hairdos and overdone makeup, made friends by the millions.

Viewers considered them "good people," hardworking, red-blooded Americans just like them. They liked the Bakkers so much, they sent them money. Whatever the Bakkers sold, the viewers bought, whether it was contributions to the ministry or vacation shares in Heritage USA, a North Carolina retreat.

Bakker was on top of his game for the longest time, then everything he had worked so hard for started to come apart. In 1978, it was disclosed that Bakker had had a sexual encounter with former church secretary Jessica Hahn (who subsequently posed nude for *Playboy* and later enjoyed minor celebrity as one of Howard Stern's hangers-on).

When it was discovered that he had paid Hahn more than two hundred thousand dollars of ministry money to keep her quiet, federal agents began an investigation of PTL Ministries. They found that he had oversold vacation shares in Heritage USA and bilked thousands of followers out of an estimated $158 million.

For his sins, Bakker was divorced by his wife, Tammy Faye, and sent to a federal prison by an unforgiving judge, where he served four and a half years. Upon his release in 1996, he rented a North Carolina farmhouse and wrote his autobiography, titled *I Was Wrong,* then moved the following year to Los Angeles, where he resided in a Christian home for addicts and gang members.

Jim Bakker has been apologizing for years for his mistakes.

Those apologies took on a more evangelistic tone following his release from prison, as he traveled the country offering guest sermons to interested congregations. He found ways to compare himself to Jesus Christ, who was wronged for doing right things.

There are few things Christians like better than hearing the testimony of a redeemed sinner or a wronged believer. Bakker offered them both.

"I believe the Bible said, above all, God wants you to prosper," Bakker says in his sermon. "Well, when I went to prison, I began to study the Bible and realized Jesus Christ didn't have anything good to say about money. He called money 'the deceitfulness of riches.' He said, 'Woe unto the rich.'"

THE ANTI-APOLOGY

In a letter to a friend, written while he was still in prison, Bakker said: "I take full responsibility for my moral failure and the fall of PTL, but I did not commit the crimes I have been accused of and am in prison for."[87]

JERRY JONES
COWBOYS OWNER GETS FAMILY TO CHURCH ON TIME

Dallas Cowboys owner Jerry Jones, his coaches, and his players are normally afforded certain perks and considerations from their fellow Texans. It seems to go with the job description in Texas, where football is *everything*.

Jones takes that special relationship seriously.

A few years ago, Jones fined then head coach Barry Switzer seventy-five thousand dollars after he was arrested at the Dallas–Ft. Worth International Airport with a .36-caliber pistol in his suitcase. Switzer told authorities that he had stored the weapon in the suitcase to hide it from children visiting his home and forgot to remove it when he packed to take a trip. Jones was indignant that his coach would do such a thing.

"We have to send the message that we really do get it," said Jones. "That although you make a mistake, it still can very negatively impact a lot of people in our organization."

Unfortunately, Jones forgot his own advice.

In late August 1999, Jones was on his way to church to attend the christening of his grandson. In a second car, following the first, were his wife, his mother-in-law, and other members of his family. When the second car was pulled over for speeding, the driver of Jones's car pulled over as well.

As the police officer was questioning the driver of the second car, Jones leaped out of his vehicle and told the officer that he and his family were in a hurry. Wink, wink—this was where the perks and special considerations were supposed to kick in. They didn't. Instead, the officer told him the procedure would take only a minute.

Not satisfied with that answer, Jones jumped into the second car and drove off, leaving the driver behind to deal with the problem. The police officer radioed an alert and Jones's car was intercepted by a second patrol car, which signaled for him to stop.

Jones refused and drove to the church, where he let his family out.

Jones was arrested and taken off to jail, charged with fleeing the scene.

Later that day, at an exhibition game between the Cowboys and the Denver Broncos, a Cowboys publicist released a statement that apologized for the commotion generated over the arrest.

Jones seemed to say that he fled the scene for the good of his family. It was a reverse take on "The Devil Made Me Do It" defense. There was no mention in the statement of any fine he might have assessed himself for bringing embarrassment to the Cowboys organization.

THE ANTI-APOLOGY

"I am sorry this has become an issue. This matter occurred because of my very sincere effort to get all of my family to the christening of our grandson. I'm again very sorry this has happened."[88]

TY HERNDON

WALK IN PARK TRIPS UP COUNTRY SINGER

In 1995, Ty Herndon's career as a country singer was just taking off.

In May, the thirty-three-year-old singer's debut single, "What Mattered Most," debuted at number one on the country charts—and he was given the "new star" treatment by the media.

That June he was in Fort Worth, Texas, where he was scheduled to perform at a convention organized by the Texas Police Association. Just hours before his performance, Herndon went to a local park frequented by gay men.

An undercover police officer spotted Herndon at 7:20 P.M., walking alone in the park. When the men passed each other, according to police records, Herndon waved at the officer, then went down a trail and sat on a log. The officer followed him and engaged him in conversation.

"What do you like?" the officer asked him.

It was at that point that the singer, according to police, opened his shorts and masturbated in front of the officer. Herndon was arrested on the spot and taken to jail. When the police searched his wallet, they found 2.49 grams of methamphetamine, a controlled substance commonly known as speed. Herndon was charged with indecent exposure and drug possession, a charge that carries a two-to-ten-year prison sentence.

Herndon's arrest was front-page news in the *Nashville Tennessean* and other newspapers across the country. A month later, the indecent exposure charge was dropped in exchange for Herndon making a guilty plea on the drug charges. He spent a month at a drug rehabilitation center and was sentenced by a judge to five years probation.

Somehow Herndon's career survived.

Four months later, before a performance in Pontiac, Michigan, Herndon told a writer for the *Detroit Free Press* that he thought, at the time of his arrest, that his career was over. Said the singer: "I'll be the first to tell you—I'm a walking miracle today."[89]

THE ANTI-APOLOGY

While he was in rehab, Herndon left a message on his answering machine:

"I'm going to be away for about a month here, dealing with personal problems. As for the charges that were brought against me, that's absolutely a bunch of [expletive]. . . . The moral of the story is, don't take a leak in the woods, because it can get you arrested."

Later, Herndon apologized for any embarrassment that his arrest might have caused his fans, but he steadfastly denied police accusations that he had exposed himself. The only reason he was in that park, he said, was to take a leak.

THE STALKER
JERRY LEWIS SEES NOTHING FUNNY ABOUT IT

It all began when comedian Jerry Lewis learned that Gary Benson, the man who had wed his housekeeper in 1989, had a criminal record. Lewis told the housekeeper about her husband's past. A year later, the couple divorced.

Over the next several years, Benson followed Lewis to his home and office, where he once allegedly displayed a gun and threatened to kill both Lewis and his seven-year-old daughter. Benson, a middle-aged man who has been diagnosed with chronic schizophrenia, also repeatedly telephoned Lewis.

As a result of those actions, Benson was convicted in 1995 of aggravated stalking and sentenced to the maximum six-year sentence. When Lewis learned that Benson would be released in early 1999, he went before the Nevada Assembly to plea for tougher stalking laws.

"Stalking has turned my life and my seven-year-old's life upside down and inside out," Lewis told the lawmakers. "I have spent $180,000 in a six-week period keeping my daughter safe. Sending her to school . . . with security. My home looked like Beirut. We had SWAT teams . . . we had helicopters, we had the FBI and Metro [police]."

Lewis said he expected Benson to resume his stalking when released.

When he learned of Lewis's concern over his release, Benson telephoned the television show *Inside Edition* from prison to talk about the comedian's concerns.

THE ANTI-APOLOGY

"I apologize and it'll never happen again," he said.

Benson admitted calling Lewis about twelve times, but he said he didn't realize his actions would have such an impact on the comedian. Then, seemingly taking away what he had granted with his apology, he said, "I didn't think I did anything."[90]

Chapter 9

"What I Did Was Wrong—But I'm Not Sorry"

GRACE SLICK
WHAT'S A LITTLE LSD AMONG FRIENDS?

In her day, Grace Slick was quite the righteous babe.

As the lead singer of Jefferson Airplane ("Somebody to Love" and "White Rabbit"), she was the undisputed Rock Diva of the 1960s and early 1970s. She was to the counterculture what President Richard Nixon was to the establishment.

Once, Slick wore a Hitler outfit to a Jefferson Airplane performance at the Fillmore East in New York, where her friend actor Rip Torn joined her onstage dressed as Nixon. Actually, Slick and the President had something in common: She and Nixon's daughter, Tricia, had attended the same upper-crust school, Finch College. As a result, Slick received an invitation to a White House tea that was held for graduates of Tricia's alma mater. In her RSVP, she identified her escort as a Mr. Leonard Haufman. Of course, Haufman was actually Abbie Hoffman, one of the most notorious and hated (by the establishment) of all the New Left Yippies who had taken to the streets to protest Nixon's Vietnam War policy.

To celebrate the occasion, Slick and Hoffman decided to slip Tricky Dick a little LSD during the festivities. "The plan was for me to reach my overly long pinky fingernail, grown especially for easy cocaine snorting, into my pocket, filled with six hundred mics of pure powdered LSD, and with a large entertainer's gesture, drop the acid into Tricky Dick's teacup," Slick recalled in her autobiography, *Somebody to Love.* "If I missed, Abbie was my backup."

Fortunately, the plan fell through when Slick and Hoffman were turned away by the Secret Service at the front door. "Look," one of the guards said. "We know you're Grace Slick, and we consider you a security risk. You're on the FBI list."

THE ANTI-APOLOGY

"I'll concede now, the LSD thing was an irresponsible and dangerous plot," Slick admitted twenty years later. "At the time, though, we were so fired up about Vietnam, so incensed that some pitiful malformation of mental functions was making the old men in power assume we should kill our young, able-bodied boys for no reason, we didn't care what it took to get the president's attention. We'd hoped that after he got through acting crazy, Tricky might contemplate his navel for six hours and decide that government just wasn't the way to go."[91]

TAMMY WYNETTE

"NO ONE WILL EVER SEE THIS BUT ME"

With hits such as "Stand By Your Man" and "D-I-V-O-R-C-E," Tammy Wynette entered the country music pantheon of greatness without a dissenting voice. At the time of her mysterious death in 1999, she had evolved into a genuine country music legend, an honor she carried with honor and dignity right up until the end of her life.

For Tammy, reigning as the Queen of Country Music was a piece of cake. It was getting there that was the bitch, for throughout the early days of her career she was hotly pursued by every male in the business, even by her own husbands (who just didn't seem to know when to quit the chase), and protecting her simmering sexuality seemed to require uncommon diligence on her part.

Once, during her marriage to Don Chapel (her second), she stepped out of the shower to find her husband with a camera at the ready. As she reached for a towel, he snapped a picture of his lovely—and completely nude—wife.

"Cut it out!" said Tammy, laughing at his sneak attack.

"Oh, don't be such a prude," he said. "I like to take pictures of you, and no one will ever see this but me."

More sneak attacks followed. It got to the point that whenever Don entered a room in which Tammy was undressing, he reached for his camera. For Tammy, the final straw occurred when she disrobed to do exercises on the floor and was captured in the act by Don and his relentless camera. Amusement on her part quickly turned to annoyance. After that incident, she locked the door whenever she wanted to undress or have privacy.

Tammy pretty much put Don's zeal out of mind. However, several months after the shower incident, she was performing at the Edison Hotel in Toronto, Ontario, when she noticed a balding man who stepped to the front of the crowd and stared at her with a smug look on his face. She noticed he had an envelope sticking out of his shirt pocket.

After the song was over, several people handed her written requests, Tammy recalled in her autobiography. "Then he [the balding man] reached forward and handed me the envelope he'd taken from his shirt. He said, 'Read this while you're on break.' I laid it on the top of the amplifier with the other requests, and when I'd finished my last song, I grabbed them all and left the stage."

As Tammy sat down at a nearby table to read the notes, Don left to fetch her a soft drink. While he was gone, she opened the envelope from the balding man with the inexplicably smug look on his face. To her horror, out tumbled a nude photograph of her stepping out of her shower.

Tammy dashed into the rest room and cried her eyes out.

Once she pulled herself together, she left the rest room and went back onstage for the second half of her show. "The man who had handed me the picture stayed in front of the bandstand, dancing with a young girl throughout the whole show, and I was so embarrassed I couldn't concentrate on performing," she later recalled. "He kept looking at me and grinning, and I wanted to jump down off the stage and slap his face."

Tammy accepted her husband's apology, but she made up her mind that the marriage was over. Before Don could say cheese, she divorced him and married country legend George Jones, who promised to love, cherish, and *not* take nude photos of his beautiful wife.

THE ANTI-APOLOGY

After the show, Tammy retreated to her tour bus, obviously upset, with Don following close behind. "When I confronted him with the picture, he was very nonchalant about the whole thing," she wrote in her autobiography.

"Oh, that's just a little hobby of mine," he explained. "I get names out of ads in porno magazines, and we swap pictures. What difference does it make? Your name's not on the picture. No one could ever prove it was you."

Tammy ripped the photograph to shreds.

"What kind of man would show other men nude pictures of his wife?" she asked.

Don didn't have a good answer.

Finally, after hearing all of Tammy's arguments about why what he had done was a dirty, low-down thing to do, Don offered her an apology and promised to destroy all the remaining photographs and negatives.[92]

DOLLY PARTON
THE BIGGER THEY ARE, THE HARDER THEY FALL

Dolly Parton has unruly breasts.

Once she and manager Sandy Gallen were having lunch in a fashionable restaurant, when the country music superstar unbuttoned her blouse and plopped her famous breasts down on a platter on the edge of the table.

"Here you go, Sandy," she said. "I'm laying 'em out for you."

Dolly thought that was pretty funny. It's not known if the waiter attempted to clear the table.

On another occasion, during the filming of the movie *Nine to Five*, Dolly was in a limo with several of her assistants and friends on the way back to the Bel Air Hotel. As they passed Welsh pop singer Tom Jones's house, Dolly wondered aloud what he would do if she got stark naked and ran across his lawn.

The limo audience dared her to do it.

"Oh, I couldn't," she said.

Then came the dreaded "double dare" challenge.

That was more than Dolly could resist. Words like "double dare" make her lose control. "It's that same kind of thing that would make a kid cut her own hair or shave her eyebrows off with her daddy's razor," she explains.

She directed the limo driver to turn around and return to Tom Jones's house. In the blink of an eye, she stripped and dashed across the singer's lawn, completely nude.

"Before I knew what was happening, I felt the cool grass of Tom Jones's yard on my bare feet," Dolly recalled. "Of course, that was a perfect complement to my bare ass parading around in the swankiest part of L.A. for all to see."

As quickly as she had jumped out of the limo, she jumped back inside.

"I got back in the car, grass-stained, guilt-stained, and feeling wicked. I don't know if Tom Jones saw me that night. I do know that shortly after that he put up a large wall around his property."

Both the boob-on-a-platter story and the streaking incident were told by Dolly in her autobiography. At the end of the book, she was given an opportunity to apologize for the explicitness of her storytelling.

THE ANTI-APOLOGY

"If I have offended anybody with any of my language," Dolly answered, "all I can say is 'tough titty.'"[93]

TANYA TUCKER
STONE-COUNTRY BAD GIRL FLASHES RADIO JOCKS

No one in country music has ever accused Tanya Tucker of shyness.

In the early years of her career—her first hit, "Delta Dawn," was recorded when she was only thirteen—she was country music's lil' sweetheart. Adults encouraged her to "speak up" and strut her stuff. They thought it was cute to see a little girl act like a grown-up woman.

Trouble is, when she hit twenty-one going on thirty, she slapped that behavior into high gear and applied those childhood encouragements to her life as an adult. Sometimes it got her in trouble. Throughout it all, she remained Nashville's lil' sweetheart despite occasionally playing a starring role as a Tabloid Queen.

In the spring of 1997, at the ripe old age of thirty-eight, Tanya proved she is still a dangerous commodity. NBC TV anchor Stone Phillips was in Nashville with a *Dateline* production crew to do a feature on Tucker.

Also in town was a convention of radio program directors.

After wrapping up the segment for *Dateline*, Tucker and Phillips went out to dinner. Then, after a few drinks, they stopped by a Printers Ally nightclub, where a record company was having a party for the visiting program directors.

Tucker and Phillips were at the nightclub only a few minutes, when Tucker jumped up on the stage between performances by Ty Herndon and Joe Diffie. To everyone's surprise, she seized the microphone and, after making an off-color remark about Herndon, who had been arrested several years earlier for flashing his penis at an undercover police officer, she lifted up her blouse and flashed the program directors with her bare breasts, which, it is said, are perfectly shaped.

There is no record of what she said at that point, but it must have been titillating. Unfortunately, the *Dateline* crew had returned to the hotel and neither of Nashville's daily newspapers had a photographer on the scene.

Tucker escaped, unscathed—or so she thought.

Radio program directors are not by nature a taciturn lot.

THE ANTI-APOLOGY

"Oh, Lord, why did I go out with Stone Phillips, why?" she moaned to a writer for *The Tennessean*. "What was I thinking?" Asked how much of the evening she recalled, she replied that, unfortunately, "I can remember all of it." Then she shrugged and said, "Oh, well, I told [Phillips] I'd show him a good time, and I showed him two of 'em."

Shortly after the incident, she went on Oprah Winfrey's show to talk about her new album, aptly titled *Complicated*. When Oprah asked her about the bare-breast display, Tucker confirmed it. Yep, she said, she showed "both of them."

To *Newsweek*, she said it was "one of those fun, fun nights that had to be spoiled by the crap."[94]

If a beautiful woman shows them her breasts, they *will* talk about it. The day following the nightclub incident, the airwaves buzzed with comments about Tucker's unexpected exposure. Some say her records experienced a surge in airplay for days after the event.

Of course, all that talk meant Tucker had to apologize.

ROB LOWE
ACTOR SPIKES CAREER WITH X-RATED SEX TAPE

Most of the stories coming out of the 1988 Democratic Convention in Atlanta were pretty tame. There were no riots, no police charges into crowds of teenagers. It was as peaceful as a Sunday picnic.

Actor Rob Lowe changed all that.

As a member of the much-publicized Hollywood "Brat Pack" of the early 1980s, a group that consisted of himself, Sean Penn, Emilio Estevez, Ally Sheedy, Molly Ringwald, and others, he had garnered a reputation for behavior that sometimes exceeded the norm.

Fans of the actor were not surprised to see him in trouble from time to time, but no one was really prepared for what happened in Atlanta, where Lowe taped himself having sex with a minor during the convention. Somehow, the film found its way into the hands of the media.

In the weeks that followed, Lowe was slapped with a civil lawsuit by the girl's mother and a Georgia district attorney let it be known that he was considering charging the actor with the sexual exploitation of a minor, a charge that could have gotten the actor twenty years in prison.

When the dust cleared, Lowe was left standing, but just barely. He escaped a prison sentence, but he was ordered to perform twenty hours of community service. For years after the event, Lowe's movie career was in a shambles.

Not until 1997, when he portrayed the head of the Christian Coalition in the movie *Contact,* was he able to regain his status as a serious movie actor.

It was always Lowe's position that whatever he did in private was his own business, even if it involved underaged girls.

THE ANTI-APOLOGY

"I simply had a lapse. I'm not asking for forgiveness. I don't need to be forgiven."

It was an unfortunate thing to have happen, he said, but nothing he should apologize for. "It was just one of those quirky, sort of naughty, sort of wild, sort of, you know, drunken things that people will do from time to time."

As the months went by—and his career opportunities seemed to shrink on a daily basis—Lowe softened his attitude somewhat.

"Everyone has an Achilles' heel, everybody has a judgment day. What I'm saying is, don't judge me by my obstacle. Judge me on how well I overcome it."[95]

Endnotes

1. *Cincinnati Enquirer* (June 28, 1998); *Newsweek* (July 13, 1998); *The Wall Street Journal* (July 17, 1998).
2. *Newsweek* (June 22, 1998 and July 20, 1998); American Forces Press Service.
3. *Newsweek* (August 3, 1998; August 17, 1998).
4. *Hello!* (April 1997); *USA Today* (March 18, 1999); MrShowbiz.com (April 17, 1997).
5. Associated Press (August 27, 1997); *Branson News,* by Susan Klopfer (1997).
6. Associated Press (September 23, 1999).
7. *Newsweek* (August 17, 1998); *The Washington Post* (December 12, 1997).
8. *The Washington Post* (May 18, 1999).
9. *London Telegraph* (October 30, 1998).
10. *Lucy: The Real Life of Lucille Ball* by Charles Higham (New York: St. Martin's Press, 1986).
11. "Elvis Presley," *Delta Democrat-Times* (August 15, 1977); "More on Elvis," *Delta Democrat-Times* (August 21, 1977).
12. *Newsweek* (June 30, 1997); *Globe* (January 16, 1997).
13. *The Lives of Norman Mailer* by Carl Rollyson (New York: Paragon House, 1991); *Playboy* (January 1968); *Newsweek* (December 9, 1968).
14. Associated Press (December 11, 1998).
15. *Los Angeles Times* (July 19, 1998).
16. MrShowbiz.com.
17. *USA Today* (February 8, 1999); *Entertainment Weekly* (September 3, 1999); Liz Smith, *Los Angeles Times* (August 10, 1999).
18. *Playboy* (October 1998), pp. 120–122; *US* (August 1999), pp.73–75.
19. *London Telegraph* (April 16, 1998).
20. *Newsweek* (January 11, 1999); ABC News Internet Ventures.
21. *USA Today* (September 29, 1999); *Maxim* (October 1999); *New York Daily News* (September 39, 1999).
22. *The First Time* by Cher (New York: Simon & Schuster, 1998), pp. 221–222.
23. *Rolling Stone* (December 10, 1998); *Entertainment Weekly* (March 27, 1998).
24. *US* (August 1999 and May 1998).
25. Associated Press (October 21, 1999); *Los Angeles Times* (February 5, 1999).
26. *Philadelphia Inquirer* (July 11, 1995); *Entertainment Weekly* (August 13, 1999).

27. *Playboy* (May 1999); MrShowbiz.com.
28. *New York Post* (August 5, 1999); ABC News Internet Ventures; *US* (July 1998).
29. Associated Press (April 23, 1999); *Los Angeles Times* (May 11, 1999; April 23, 1999).
30. *Esquire* (April 1994), pp. 96–97.
31. Associated Press (October 21, 1999); E! Online (January 7, 1997).
32. *The Real Bettie Page* by Richard Foster (Birch Lane Press, 1997).
33. *Newsweek* (June 14, 1999); CNN (September 4, 1997); Newsweek Online.
34. Associated Press reports; CBS 2 News in Los Angeles.
35. *Ashbury Park Press* (August 21, 1998).
36. *Wyatt Earp: The Life Behind the Legend* by Casey Tefertiller (New York: John Wiley & Sons, 1997).
37. *Newsweek* (October 19, 1998); ABC-TV interview with Barbara Walters.
38. *Butch Cassidy: A Biography* by Richard Patterson (Lincoln, Nebraska: University of Nebraska Press, 1998).
39. *Newsweek* (August 4, 1997); MrShowbiz.com.
40. *US* magazine (August 1998); *USA Today* (June 19, 1995); *Philadelphia Inquirer* (June 17, 1995).
41. *Marilyn* by Norman Mailer (New York: Grosset and Dunlap, 1973); *Marilyn Monroe* by Donald Spoto (New York: HarperCollins, 1993); *Norma Jean* by Fred Lawrence Guiles (New York: McGraw-Hill, 1969); *Marilyn: The Last Take* by Peter Brown and Patte B. Barham (New York: Dutton, 1992).
42. *I Lived to Tell It All* by George Jones with Tom Carter (New York: Villard, 1996).
43. *Philadelphia Inquirer* (July 24, 1984); Official Miss America Web site.
44. The author, James L. Dickerson, is the reporter in this story.
45. *Newsweek* (November 8, 1999); Associated Press (October 6, 1997); *Entertainment Weekly* (July 11, 1997).
46. *London Telegraph* (September 25, 1996).
47. *Los Angeles Times* (June 24, 1999); *Entertainment Weekly* (April 30, 1999).
48. Associated Press (October 12, 1999); ABC News Internet Ventures; *Extra* (October 11, 1998).
49. *Sarah, The Duchess of York* by Sarah Ferguson with Jeff Coplon (New York: Simon & Schuster, 1996).
50. *Garth Brooks: One of a Kind, Workin' on a Full House* by Rick Mitchell (New York: Fireside, 1993); *Three Chords and the Truth* by Laurence Leamer (New York: HarperCollins, 1997).
51. *The Star* (1999); Associated Press (November 20, 1999).

52. *Many Years From Now* by Barry Miles (New York: Henry Holt, 1997).
53. Associated Press (September 16, 1999); CNN interview; Associated Press (April 9, 1998).
54. *Rolling Stone* (October 15, 1998).
55. Associated Press (August 19, 1999); *Boston Herald* (August 18, 1999).
56. *The Washington Post* (January 4, 1992; March 15, 1990).
57. *To Seek a Newer World* by Robert Kennedy (New York: Bantam, 1968).
58. *London Telegraph* (November 22, 1994).
59. *Newsweek* (October 25, 1999); Associated Press (October 19, 1999; August 24, 1999); Channel 4000.
60. *The Rape of Nanking* by Iris Chang (New York: Basic Books, 1997).
61. Associated Press (September 7, 1999); *Entertainment Weekly* (October 29, 1999); *Newsweek* (October 24, 1988).
62. *The Washington Post* (1990); *Playboy* (October 1991).
63. National Gay and Lesbian Task Force press release (January 27, 1995); *Atlanta Constitution* (July 13, 1995).
64. Associated Press (October 26, 1999).
65. *Behind the Oval Office* by Dick Morris (New York: Random House, 1997); *Los Angeles Times* (August 31, 1996).
66. "This Show Is Good for America," *Rolling Stone* (May 14, 1998); Playboy Interview, *Playboy* (July 1998).
67. *The Washington Post* (February 8, 1998); Free Press News Services (February 6, 1998); Fox Television interview.
68. *The Washington Post* (February 1, 1999); United Press International (March 2, 1999).
69. Associated Press (December 23, 1999); Associated Press (March 2, 2000); *The Clarion-Ledger*, Jackson, Mississippi (December 27, 1999); Associated Press (April 21, 2000).
70. *Newsweek* (July 27, 1998); *Facts on File*; *Time* (October 6, 1997); *Sports Illustrated* (October 6, 1997).
71. *Larry King Live*, CNN; *Miami Herald* (June 23, 1999).
72. Associated Press (November 3, 1998); CNN broadcast of Kerry Collins's press conference.
73. Associated Press (November 23, 1999).
74. *Atlanta Journal-Constitution* (October 22, 1998); the Morris News Service.
75. *The Washington Post* (May 23, 1998).
76. Associated Press (December 14, 1998).
77. Associated Press (November 5, 1998).

78. *Miami Herald* (October 27, 1997); Associated Press (June 26, 1998).
79. *Jet* (January 26, 1998); *Time* (July 14, 1997); *Playboy* (November 1998).
80. Associated Press (June 13, 1997); CBS Sportsline (June 9, 1997).
81. Associated Press (April 25, 1997); *Golf Magazine* Online (April 24, 1997).
82. *Los Angeles Times* (June 21, 1995); *Atlanta Constitution* (June 21, 1995).
83. Associated Press (March 13, 2000); Associated Press (March 11, 2000); Associated Press (March 12, 2000).
84. Nashville *Tennessean* (January 21, 2000); *The Tennessean* (July 5, 1999); Nashville *Tennessean* (June 18, 1999).
85. "Still Wrestling with the Devil," *Christianity Today* (March 2, 1998); "TV Preachers on the Rocks," *Newsweek* (July 11, 1988); "Worshipers on a Holy Roll," *Time* (April 11, 1988).
86. *Facts on File World News* CD-ROM (September 7, 1995); www.capitolhill-blue.org
87. *The Washington Post* (August 11, 1999); *Los Angeles Times* (March 2, 1996).
88. *Associated Press* (August 29, 1999).
89. *Detroit Free Press* (September 8, 1995); *The Tennessean* (June 15, 1995); *People* (July 3, 1995).
90. *Las Vegas Sun* (March 11, 1999); Associated Press (September 23, 1999).
91. *Somebody to Love* by Grace Slick with Andrea Cagan (New York: Warner Books, 1998).
92. *Stand By Your Man* by Tammy Wynette (New York: Simon & Schuster, 1979), pp. 128–130.
93. *Dolly: My Life and Other Unfinished Business* by Dolly Parton (New York: HarperCollins, 1994).
94. *Newsweek* (April 14, 1997); *The Tennessean* (April 6, 1997); *Los Angeles Times* (April 2, 1997).
95. *Miami Herald* (March 7, 1990); ABC News Internet Ventures.

Index